W9-DAI-778

HEALTHY MEAL PREP SLOW COOKER COOKBOOK

Healthy Meal Prep

Slow Cooker Cookbook

Nutritious Recipes
to Prep Ahead and
Enjoy All Week

Lauren Keating

Photography by Antonis Achilleos

ROCKRIDGE
PRESS

Copyright © 2020 by Rockridge Press, Emeryville, California

No part of this publication may be reproduced, stored in a retrieval system, or transmitted in any form or by any means, electronic, mechanical, photocopying, recording, scanning, or otherwise, except as permitted under Sections 107 or 108 of the 1976 United States Copyright Act, without the prior written permission of the Publisher. Requests to the Publisher for permission should be addressed to the Permissions Department, Rockridge Press, 6005 Shellmound Street, Suite 175, Emeryville, CA 94608.

Limit of Liability/Disclaimer of Warranty: The Publisher and the author make no representations or warranties with respect to the accuracy or completeness of the contents of this work and specifically disclaim all warranties, including without limitation warranties of fitness for a particular purpose. No warranty may be created or extended by sales or promotional materials. The advice and strategies contained herein may not be suitable for every situation. This work is sold with the understanding that the Publisher is not engaged in rendering medical, legal, or other professional advice or services. If professional assistance is required, the services of a competent professional person should be sought. Neither the Publisher nor the author shall be liable for damages arising herefrom. The fact that an individual, organization, or website is referred to in this work as a citation and/or potential source of further information does not mean that the author or the Publisher endorses the information the individual, organization, or website may provide or recommendations they/it may make. Further, readers should be aware that websites listed in this work may have changed or disappeared between when this work was written and when it is read.

For general information on our other products and services or to obtain technical support, please contact our Customer Care Department within the United States at (866) 744-2665, or outside the United States at (510) 253-0500.

Rockridge Press publishes its books in a variety of electronic and print formats. Some content that appears in print may not be available in electronic books, and vice versa.

TRADEMARKS: Rockridge Press and the Rockridge Press logo are trademarks or registered trademarks of Callisto Media Inc. and/or its affiliates, in the United States and other countries, and may not be used without written permission. All other trademarks are the property of their respective owners. Rockridge Press is not associated with any product or vendor mentioned in this book.

Interior and Cover Designer: Rachel Haeseker
Art Producer: Meg Baggott
Editor: Rachel Feldman
Production Editor: Rachel Taenzler

Photography © 2020 Antonis Achilleos. Food styling by Rishon Hanners.

ISBN: Print 978-1-64611-888-5 | eBook 978-1-64611-889-2

R0

To everyone trying to live life, have fun, and still get a healthy dinner on the table: You've got this.

Korean-Inspired Beef Wraps
page 121

Contents

Introduction

The number one question I get from people when they find out I write a successful food blog, while also working a high-stress day job, is how on earth I have time to do all that cooking. I get it. It feels like we never have enough time to do all the things we want. And cooking is usually the first chore dropped.

But healthy eating doesn't have to take a ton of effort! I promise.

I first learned to appreciate slow cookers as a major time saver when I was in high school. Tuesday was always slow cooker night. Between taking me to school, tennis practice, and a dance class almost an hour away from home, there was no way my mom had time to cook a proper meal from scratch. So, she let the slow cooker do the work for her. That was back before the days of delivery apps—we couldn't even get a pizza delivered to our house—so it was her only option. But it worked well. Her slow cooker pot roast was usually the highlight of my week.

Fast-forward a few decades and here I am. When I started my blog, healthy-delicious.com, I had no idea what I was getting into. What started as a simple way to share tried-and-true recipes with a few friends quickly grew into a thriving business. Like so many bloggers, I entertained the dream of quitting my day job and staying home to cook all day. I even enrolled in culinary school. But the truth is, I love my day job way too much to give it up. So, here I am, still trying to balance my two passions. Trust me, if I can juggle it all, you can, too! One-pot recipes, meal planning, and slow cooker recipes have been a lifesaver for me. My first book, *Healthy Eating One-Pot Cookbook*, covered one-pot recipes, whereas this book covers meal prep and slow cooker recipes.

Slow cookers are the definition of easy cooking. Just throw a bunch of ingredients in, push the button, and walk away while it does all the work for you. Right? Well, almost. If you really want to take advantage of the convenience that slow cookers offer, you'll need to be smart about prep. Slow cookers are just that: slow cookers. It will take about 8 hours to make a meal. That means planning is crucial. This book teaches you the techniques of smart meal prep so you can maximize your time and complete kitchen tasks on a schedule that works *for* you, instead of against you.

In this book, I share 100 easy, healthy recipes for breakfast, lunch, and dinner, along with prep-ahead and handy storage tips. Armed with these strategies, you'll see how combining the benefits of meal prep with the convenience of a slow cooker can make healthy eating easier than ever, even in today's fast-paced world.

CHAPTER 1

Slow Cooking in a Fast-Paced World

I know how much of a struggle it can be to find time to cook dinner after a long day. And that's coming from someone who loves to cook!

I can't tell you how many times I've wished for a Jetsons-like robot that could make (and clean up) dinner for me. Although that may sound like a fantasy, it's actually not that far off from what's possible when you take advantage of a slow cooker.

In this chapter, I show you how to put your slow cooker to work for you, cooking dinner all day while you go about life. Dinner will be hot and ready when you're ready to eat. You might need to add a few finishing touches, but it sure beats starting from square one when you come home at the end of a long day.

I break down the basics of meal prep, my favorite strategies for prepping with a slow cooker, and helpful information on logistics, like how to store meals safely.

With the tips and recipes that follow, healthy eating couldn't be easier or more convenient.

Eating Healthy with Your Slow Cooker

When you close your eyes and think of slow cookers, what do you see?

I'd be willing to bet it's an old-fashioned image of your grandma or your favorite beef stew from childhood. Slow cookers can bring a sense of nostalgia, and in many cases, they've been pushed to the back of the closet and disregarded as newer, more modern appliances have entered the market.

It doesn't help that so many popular slow cooker recipes are full of cream-of-something soups, gobs of cheese, and heavily processed ingredients that don't fall in line with modern trends toward fresh, clean eating.

But there's definitely a place for slow cookers in a modern kitchen. People are busier than ever and looking for ways to simplify home cooking, which is exactly what slow cookers do best.

And slow cookers can be used for so much more than just creamy casseroles and hearty stews. Most people associate slow cookers with winter recipes, but they're actually amazing in summer, too—and they won't heat up your house the way your oven does. You can make everything from slow-cooked steel cut oats to quinoa-stuffed peppers to peanut chicken inspired by your favorite takeout order.

Cooking food low and slow helps tenderize lean cuts of meat and gives flavors time to develop, making it easy to reduce the amount of saturated fat in your diet without sacrificing flavor. The slow cooker's low, even temperatures also reduce the risk of burning foods. If you're concerned with the harmful compounds and free radicals that can be created when food is scorched or oil is heated beyond its smoke point, slow cookers can offer peace of mind.

Modern slow cookers are available with all sorts of bells and whistles. Some let you sauté food right in the crock, and others have temperature probes that let you know when your food is done. Some even have Bluetooth and Wi-Fi. Those features can be fun, but the two things you really want when purchasing a new slow cooker are the ability to set the timer in 30-minute increments and a "keep warm" setting that turns on after the set cooking time has run its course. That way, your food stays hot (and at a safe temperature) if you get pulled into a late meeting, go to the gym, run errands after work, or decide to meet friends for an impromptu happy hour. Because, let's face it, life happens and 9-to-5 schedules are so last century.

HEALTHY EATING PRINCIPLES

Having a game plan for the week and healthy meals prepped and ready to go makes it so much easier to stay on track and avoid takeout or shortcut meals.

But planning is only the first step. What goes into your meals is important, too.

So, what is healthy? If you ask 10 people what healthy eating looks like, you'll probably get 10 different answers. Add health conditions to the mix, such as food allergies, diabetes, or weight loss goals, and it's no wonder there is confusion.

I always try to take an inclusive approach to healthy eating, focusing on consuming a variety of nutrient-dense foods from across all food groups. A great reference is the United States Department of Health and Human Services's *Dietary Guidelines for Americans*.

The following principles guide the recipes in this book and can be applied to everyday life, too.

1. **Eat the rainbow.** Enjoy a variety of fruits and vegetables of all colors. Yellow and red vegetables are just as important as green ones. If a meal tends to be more meat or grain heavy, round it out with a simple salad or grab a piece of fruit for dessert.

2. **Focus on whole grains.** Make at least half of your grains whole grains, which are less processed and contain more fiber and nutrients than refined grains.

3. **Vary your proteins.** Eat a variety of proteins from both meat and vegetarian sources, including lean meats and poultry, seafood, beans, legumes, and nuts. Protein helps keep you feeling full, so I try to include some in every meal.

4. **Limit added sugars and saturated fat.** Sugars and saturated fats should be limited to 10 percent of your daily caloric intake. Choose unrefined sweeteners, such as fruit purees, honey, and pure maple syrup, and opt for plant-based oils, avoiding those with saturated and trans fats.

5. **Cut back on sodium.** Minimizing the amount of processed foods you eat will naturally reduce your sodium (and sugar) intake. When you use shortcut ingredients like broth, look for reduced-sodium or no-salt-added versions. That way, you control how much salt is in your final dish. According to the *Cook's Illustrated* website, draining and rinsing items such as canned beans can reduce sodium levels by more than 20 percent.

Making It Easy with Meal Prep

Slow cookers take the hassle out of cooking, but they still require some prep to bring out the best in the ingredients you put into them. Meal prep is a complete game changer when it comes to healthy eating for a busy lifestyle, so it's no surprise it's exploded in popularity.

What's nice about meal prep is it can all be done on any schedule. I'm not a morning person, so even the simplest recipes can be too much to throw together in the rush to get out the door. That's why I do most of my prep over the weekend. With everything already cut up, measured, and assembled, all I need to do in the morning is pop the ingredients into the slow cooker and turn it on. Another option is to prep in the evening on weeknights after you have a boost of energy from eating dinner. Reversing the traditional order of things—eat first, cook later—can make it feel like you've discovered a whole new world.

Combining meal prep techniques with slow cooker cooking means less time spent working in the kitchen and more time for other things.

Prep in 1, 2, 3

To get started with meal prep, you only need to follow these three steps.

1. CHOOSE THE MEALS

Think about what meals you need for the week ahead. Do you need breakfast? Will you bring lunch to work? Do you have any evening plans that mean you won't need to eat at home one night, or are friends coming over and you need to cook extra food? Once you've determined how many meals you need, flip through this book and pick out some recipes to try.

A week of chicken or curry at every meal can get boring fast, so I like to make sure I choose a variety of protein options and flavors. That way, you can switch between heartier meals and lighter ones.

I start by choosing a soup or stew, a chicken recipe, a heartier meat dish, and a vegetarian option. It can also be helpful to pay attention to ingredients that can be used in multiple meals (for example, choosing two recipes that use stew meat rather than one recipe that uses stew meat and one that uses a roast). That way, you save money buying in bulk. Or maybe it makes sense to buy a 3-pound bag of onions rather than 2 or 3 individual onions.

2. GO SHOPPING

The day before you plan to cook, check your cabinets and refrigerator to see what ingredients you already have. Then, based on the recipes you've selected, make a list of what you need and head to the grocery store. Better yet, take advantage of grocery delivery if that's available where you live. It saves a ton of time. Even with the small fee these services charge. I usually end up saving money because I am not throwing a bunch of extra items in my cart as I wander the aisles.

Depending on how crunched for time I am, I may also purchase convenience items like pre-cut squash or jarred minced garlic. They cost a little more, but sometimes it's worth it.

3. PREP FOR THE WEEK

There are so many approaches to this step. You can cook all your meals completely and reheat them during the week, prep them up to the cooking stage so you can easily put them in your slow cooker each day, or batch cook, mixing and matching your favorites to create new combinations throughout the week. I'll cover these techniques more thoroughly in the next section. You may also want to double recipes and freeze half to get a head start on easy meals weeks or months down the road.

Meal Prep Strategies for the Slow Cooker

The great thing about meal prep is that it doesn't have to look the same for everyone.

You can set aside a block of time on Sunday to prep for the whole week, but it's not unusual to find me in the kitchen at 9 o'clock or 10 o'clock at night getting things ready for the next day's meal. It all comes down to your personal style and how much time you want to commit to prep at once. All recipes in this book are meal-prep friendly, meaning they include instructions for prepping ahead, storing for the days ahead, and freezing for longer-term storage.

Prep Ahead

This is my personal favorite approach to using my slow cooker. You essentially create a from-scratch version of the processed slow cooker meals you can sometimes find in your grocer's freezer case.

When following this method, you cut your vegetables, portion your broths and seasonings, and do some light cooking. Then pack it together so you can throw it in your slow cooker when you're ready. You'll have a hot, fresh dinner waiting for you when you get home. All you'll need to do is put on a few final touches before serving.

Batch Cooking to the Rescue

Batch cooking means fully preparing a few staples you can mix and match in different ways throughout the week. This method gives you a little more flexibility to change things up on the fly depending on what you feel like eating at the moment. Chapter 7 is filled with fantastic recipes for batch cooking.

1. Cook a few items that will keep well. I recommend one protein, one starch or grain, one bean, and one vegetable recipe. Cook as much or as little of each as you want.

2. Refrigerate everything in separate containers.

3. Mix and match the pre-cooked ingredients, adding sauces, condiments, or other items from your pantry or refrigerator to make complete meals.

In practice, batch cooking looks something like this:

- Spend a day making big batches of Poached Chicken (page 140), Brown Rice (page 145), Beans (page 146), and Ratatouille (page 136). These can be used for different variations of lunch and dinner throughout the week.

- One night, add the chicken and rice to broth from your freezer to make a simple chicken and rice soup.

- For lunch the next day, prep a vegetarian rice bowl topped with beans, ratatouille, and pesto, or shred the chicken and mix it with hot sauce and beans for a quick Buffalo chicken chili.

- The next night, boil some pasta and stir in ratatouille, olive oil, and Kalamata olives for a Mediterranean-inspired meal.

- The following night, make chicken fried rice, a barbecue chicken sandwich, or a pot of beans and greens.

Your options are practically limitless and, as the staples are relatively basic, you can play around with different sauces and seasonings so it doesn't feel like you're eating the same thing all week.

Cook Once, Eat All Week

This approach is exactly what it sounds like. You cook complete meals for easy grab-and-go meals to reheat all week. For example, make a batch of Broccoli Cheddar Soup (page 41) on Saturday morning and let it cook while you run errands. When you get home, blend the soup and divide it into individual containers. On Sunday morning, mix up a batch of Apple-Cinnamon Steel Cut Oatmeal (page 21) or cook a Sausage and Broccoli Frittata (page 28) to have for breakfast for the week.

BUDGET HACKS FOR MEAL PREP

Buy from the bulk section. Self-serve supermarket sections are gold mines for saving cash. If recipes only call for half a cup of a specific nut, for example, stop by the bulk section and see whether the unit price is less expensive than the packaged version. For the same reason, if you plan to make a lot of quinoa, the bulk section is usually a better deal and involves less packaging than the boxed products.

Make friends with the freezer section. Utilizing less expensive frozen items can help cut down on buying expensive fresh produce. Bonus: Your food will last longer. Just remember to always thaw your food before you put it in the slow cooker.

Eat more plants. Meals can become more expensive if always planned around proteins like fresh meat and seafood. Canned varieties are less expensive, nonperishable, and time-saving. You can save even more money by eating vegetarian and vegan meals a few times per week, so don't skip chapter 4.

SAMPLE MEAL PREP PLAN

With a little bit of planning and organization, it only takes 2 to 3 hours of hands-on time to cook breakfast, whip up a batch of soup for lunches, and prep your Monday through Thursday dinners so all you'll need to do is throw them in the slow cooker in the morning.

Planning also helps save money: Purchase chicken breasts in bulk to use in both the soup and the chicken dinner. Because meat doesn't keep well in the refrigerator for more than a few days, I cook those recipes earlier in the week.

You can even plan further into the future by making a double batch and freezing half or spending a weekend cooking a few recipes to freeze for later.

	BREAKFAST	LUNCH	DINNER
Day 1	Cherry-Almond Granola (page 20) with yogurt	Chicken and Wild Rice Soup (page 49)	Thai-Inspired Barbecue Meatloaf (page 123)
Day 2	Cherry-Almond Granola (leftovers) with yogurt	Chicken and Wild Rice Soup (leftovers)	Lemon Chicken (page 88)
Day 3	Cherry-Almond Granola (leftovers) with yogurt	Lemon Chicken (leftovers)	Butternut Squash Macaroni and Cheese (page 75)
Day 4	Cherry-Almond Granola (leftovers) with yogurt	Butternut Squash Macaroni and Cheese (leftovers)	Tex-Mex Quinoa (page 66)
Day 5	Cherry-Almond Granola (leftovers) with yogurt	Tex-Mex Quinoa (leftovers)	Take out!

STEP-BY-STEP PREP

1. Sunday morning: Prep and cook Chicken and Wild Rice Soup (page 49). Depending on what your day looks like, cook this on Low heat for 8 hours while you run errands, or High heat for 4 hours so that it's done faster. Portion the cooked soup into individual containers for lunches during the week.

2. Clean your slow cooker and prepare a batch of Cherry-Almond Granola (page 20) to eat with yogurt for breakfast all week.

3. While the granola cooks, prepare your dinners. Start by gathering several containers to store your prepped foods. For this menu, you'll need two large, sturdy containers (one for the meatloaf and one for the macaroni and cheese), one medium container or Mason jar for the quinoa ingredients, and one storage bag for the lemon chicken.

4. Gather and prep the produce.

5. Sauté any vegetables, as needed. (For this menu, skip this step.)

6. Cook any meat as instructed by the recipes. (Again, this step can be skipped for this menu, since none call for this.)

7. Pack the ingredients into separate containers, following the prep ahead instructions provided.

8. To make mornings as easy as possible, clearly label everything with the recipe name and the day you plan to cook it. If you double any recipes to freeze, label them with the recipe name, the creation date, and the cook-by date.

9. Put everything in the refrigerator. Sit down and put your feet up. You deserve it!

Your Kitchen Necessities

Stocking your kitchen with healthy basics will go a long way toward setting you up for success. I include some of my personal favorites here—items I use frequently in my kitchen and throughout this book. Think of it as a starting guide, which you can add to or delete from according to your personal taste and cooking style.

Go-To Ingredients

Following are my go-to ingredients—the ones I reach for time and again to make sure my slow cooker meals are packed with flavor.

SPICE RACK

Dried herbs and spices are a great way to add flavor to recipes. My spice collection is massive, but these are a few of my favorites. Remember, when it comes to slow cooker recipes, you'll need more seasoning than when cooking on the stovetop, because the moist cooking environment can dilute the flavors.

- **Cinnamon:** This spice goes into a lot of my breakfast recipes, but it's great in savory recipes, too.

- **Cumin:** This is a staple for both Mexican- and Indian-inspired recipes.

- **Italian seasoning blend:** This versatile staple can add flavor to a wide variety of recipes.

- **Red curry paste:** This ingredient is an easy addition for tons of flavor to Southeast Asian–inspired recipes.

PANTRY

A well-stocked pantry means you're never far from a delicious, home-cooked meal. These ingredients often create the backbone of a recipe, giving it structure and flavor. Some recipes can even be made entirely with pantry staples.

- **Canned beans:** I keep canned beans handy, because I don't always feel like cooking dried beans from scratch.

- **Cornstarch:** I don't use cornstarch often when I cook on the stove, but it's useful for thickening sauces and gravies in the slow cooker. Just mix in 1 to 2 tablespoons before serving and watch that thin cooking liquid transform into a rich, glossy sauce.

- **Fire-roasted canned tomatoes (crushed and diced):** Regular tomatoes are great, but I love the extra dimension fire-roasted tomatoes give slow cooker meals.

- **Honey:** This is my preferred sweetener. I buy local varieties whenever I can.

- **Low-sodium chicken stock:** Most slow cooker recipes require at least a splash of liquid. This is my go-to.

- **Mustard:** Acidic ingredients like mustard perk up slow cooker recipes and keep the flavors from tasting muddy.

- **Shallots:** Shallots are milder and a little sweeter than yellow onions, so I find they work better when thrown into the slow cooker raw. They also have a subtle garlic flavor, so they can pull double duty in a pinch.

- **Worcestershire sauce:** This sauce adds depth of flavor to beefy recipes.

REFRIGERATOR AND FREEZER

Here are several items usually found in my refrigerator and freezer. I restock these ingredients just about every time I go to the grocery store.

- **Baby spinach:** If you want to eat more vegetables, there aren't many recipes that won't benefit from a handful of fresh baby spinach. You can also use it to make a simple salad.

- **Citrus fruits:** A squeeze of fresh citrus juice can really perk up the flavors of slow-cooked foods.

- **Fat-free Greek yogurt:** A scoop of yogurt stirred into a soup or spooned onto a casserole can add richness.

- **Fresh salsa:** This is my favorite shortcut ingredient! There are so many times you can use fresh salsa instead of chopping tomatoes, peppers, and onions separately.

- **Tortillas (corn or grain-free):** Leftovers don't seem as boring when you turn them into a taco.

- **Zucchini:** This squash can be cut into all kinds of shapes, from big chunks to delicate noodles.

Handy Tools and Equipment

In addition to a slow cooker itself, consider having these basic kitchen tools on hand.

- **Immersion blender:** This appliance is great for blending soups right in the slow cooker.

- **Instant-read thermometer:** This helps you know when bigger cuts of meat or baked goods are cooked properly.

- **Kitchen towels:** Placing a clean kitchen towel under the lid of your slow cooker traps condensation and prevents meals from getting soupy or soggy.

- **Slow cooker liners:** This is helpful for easy cleanup. You can buy disposable liners or reusable silicone ones.

- **Tongs:** Use these to easily transfer items to and from your slow cooker.

SLOW COOKER PREP SECRETS

1. **Get to know your slow cooker.** Cooking times can vary slightly from slow cooker to slow cooker. Do a few tests before leaving yours unattended all day—you don't want burned food if your cooker runs hot.

2. **If flavor matters, sauté. If time matters, microwave.** I recommend sautéing aromatics such as onion and garlic before adding them to the slow cooker because they'll start to caramelize and take on some sweetness. If time is an issue, microwave them for a minute to soften, or just throw them into your cooker raw.

3. **Don't open the lid.** Every time you open the lid, you add 20 to 30 minutes to the total cooking time. Unless the instructions specifically call for it, only remove the lid 30 to 45 minutes before you expect your food to be done.

4. **Season generously.** When you cook on the stovetop, liquid evaporates and flavors concentrate. That doesn't happen in a slow cooker. In fact, meats and vegetables often add liquid to the dish as they cook. To ensure the flavor of your recipe isn't diluted, add about 50 percent more seasoning than you might typically use.

5. **Add delicate ingredients and dairy at the end.** Delicate ingredients like zucchini and fresh herbs can break down if they cook all day long. Similarly, dairy can curdle when cooked too long. Add these ingredients in the last 30 minutes or so of cooking. They'll have plenty of time to warm up and add flavor.

6. **Never add frozen ingredients to your slow cooker.** Slow cookers are designed to heat up slowly. Frozen food, especially large cuts of meat, may not heat up fast enough, spending too much time in the food safety tempera-ture "danger zone." Always thaw meat, or any frozen food, overnight in the refrigerator before adding it to your slow cooker.

The Art of Storage

When you embark on your meal prep journey, you'll quickly learn you can never have too many storage options. From big bags to hold prepped ingredients waiting to be cooked to individual-portion containers for grab-and-go meals, storage containers are the MVPs of meal prep.

Storage Containers

Storage containers are the workhorses of meal prep, so stock a variety of options in multiple sizes to choose from. Look for those that offer tight-fitting, leak-free lids and are microwave, freezer, and dishwasher safe.

- **BPA-free plastic:** Plastic containers are more affordable, stack neatly for easy storage, and are lighter to carry, but they're prone to staining and don't always hold up well. Ziploc, Glad, and Rubbermaid make affordable options you can find in most major grocery stores. Rigid containers are great for storing leftovers, but I also love using gallon-size zip-top bags for keeping raw ingredients organized. When possible, purchase plastic that is BPA-free; BPA omits a compound that is known to interfere with human hormones and health.

- **Glass:** Glass looks nice, is durable, and is the more environmentally friendly option, but it can be heavy and take up a lot of storage space. I like Pyrex and the multi-compartment PrepNaturals containers found on Amazon.

- **Mason jars:** These are great for soups, salads, oatmeal, and breakfast parfaits.

- **Stackable:** If you're short on space, look for stackable containers, which take up less room when not in use. I like to buy deli cups in various sizes online or at a restaurant supply store. In addition to nesting together neatly, one size top fits multiple sizes of containers, so you're never stuck searching for the right lid.

Smart Labeling

Labeling containers with the contents and date is important when you're working with so many recipes at once. Some recipes can look similar, so it can be hard to tell what's in the container. And if you're cooking for people with different dietary needs, you don't have room for ambiguity. Get fancy with a label maker or an erasable marker, or take a cue from restaurant kitchens and use masking tape and a marker.

Thawing and Reheating

Once packaged, food should be stored only as long as indicated in the recipe, or according to general food safety guidelines. For more information, refer to StillTasty.com and Foodsafety.gov for its FoodKeeper app.

Reheat only as much food as you plan to eat for that meal, as continually heating and cooling the same food can lead to quality issues.

Cover your food while reheating it to prevent moisture loss, and be sure to bring soups and stews to a rolling boil. Heat other recipes until they reach an internal temperature of 160°F. Microwaves tend to heat unevenly, so rotate your food and check the temperature in several spots. It's also best to microwave foods in wide, flat containers as opposed to tall, narrow jars—the food will heat more evenly because it's spread out.

What Not to Prep

The meals included in this book are designed to keep and reheat well, but some finishing touches are best saved for serving time. Fresh herbs, uncooked garnishes like sliced avocado, and splashes of lemon juice or vinegar to brighten flavors generally aren't good candidates for preparing ahead of time. Where they make sense, I've added useful tips to maximize your time. For example, lemon wedges can be refrigerated in water for several days or can be frozen for longer storage.

HOW TO STORE FOOD PROPERLY

When it comes to food safety, proper food storage is important.

Periodically check your refrigerator and freezer to ensure they're maintaining the proper temperature. Keep the refrigerator temperature at or below 40°F, and the freezer temperature at 0°F. Overfilling your refrigerator or freezer can restrict airflow and cause the temperature to rise, so clean out both on a regular basis and discard any spoiled items.

When cooking food in bulk, divide it into small containers or sealed storage bags. If you put the entire recipe in one big container, it will take longer to cool and could become unsafe to eat. Leave the container uncovered until it stops steaming, then cover tightly and refrigerate within 2 hours of cooking. Most foods will keep well in the refrigerator for 3 to 5 days. Any longer than that could cause food safety concerns, plus your meals might not be as tasty.

Freezing is great for longer-term storage. Although it doesn't kill most bacteria, it does cause it to stop growing. Food will remain safe indefinitely when kept at 0°F, but quality, including tenderness, texture, flavor, and color, will decline as time passes.

	REFRIGERATOR	FREEZER
Cooked meat (beef, chicken, pork, etc.)	3 to 4 days	4 months
Egg-based recipes (frittata, etc.)	3 to 4 days	2 months
Grains (farro, quinoa, rice)	4 to 6 days	6 months
Raw sliced vegetables	3 to 5 days	Do not freeze
Soups and stews	4 to 5 days	2 to 3 months
Stock	3 to 4 days	4 months

About the Recipes

The recipes in this book were designed to be made in a 6-quart slow cooker. If you're working with a different size, or if you just want to scale the recipes up or down, that's easy to do by multiplying or dividing the ingredient amounts. Just be sure that your slow cooker is between half and three-fourths full so it can work properly. Cooking times can be thrown off if the slow cooker is over- or underfilled.

Recipes that are meal-prep friendly. All main recipes in this book have "prep ahead" tips with instructions for prepping the meal in advance so that it's ready to be thrown in the slow cooker later in the week.

Easy recipes. Because I know no one wants to spend their entire weekend in front of the stove or doing dishes, the recipes included in this book require very little preparation time. Most recipes have fewer than 10 ingredients and do not require more than 15 minutes of hands-on prep time. Less time standing in front of the stove is always a win, if you ask me.

A chapter of recipes for batch cooking. Chapter 7 includes recipes for simple proteins, grains, beans, and vegetables that are great for making ahead to use for buffet-style meal prep. These recipes can be used on their own or mixed and matched with main recipes.

Labels for ease. To help you quickly identify the easiest recipes, I've included labels with each recipe:

- **5-Ingredient:** Not counting salt, pepper, or oil, these recipes only need 5 ingredients.

- **Freezer-Friendly:** These meals are well suited for freezing for later.

- **One-Pot:** These recipes don't require any pre-cooking, so the entire meal is prepared in your slow cooker.

- **Dietary Labels:** These indicate whether a recipe is dairy-free, gluten-free, vegan, or vegetarian.

CHAPTER 2

Breakfast

Cherry-Almond Granola

Serves 10 / Prep Time: 5 minutes / Cook Time: 2 hours (High)

DAIRY-FREE   FREEZER-FRIENDLY   ONE-POT   VEGETARIAN

If you thought slow cookers are only good for cooking soups and stews, you'll be surprised to learn you can also use them to make granola. Leaving the lid slightly ajar lets steam escape, helping the granola crisp. Egg whites help the oats form crunchy clusters, and honey adds a touch of sweetness. Once you get the hang of this recipe, it's easy to swap out the fruit and nuts to make it your own.

Nonstick cooking spray

4 cups old-fashioned rolled oats

3 large egg whites

⅓ cup honey

¼ cup unsweetened shredded coconut

½ teaspoon ground cinnamon

½ cup sliced almonds

½ cup unsweetened dried cherries

1. Generously coat your slow cooker with cooking spray and add the oats, egg whites, honey, coconut, and cinnamon. Mix well to moisten the oats thoroughly.

2. Cover the slow cooker, leaving the lid slightly ajar. Cook on High heat for 1 hour. Stir the granola to help prevent it from sticking to the bottom of the slow cooker. Re-cover the cooker and cook for 1 hour more.

3. Stir in the almonds and cherries. Turn off the slow cooker and let the granola cool completely.

4. Store individual portions in airtight containers in a cool, dry place for up to 2 weeks, or freeze for up to 3 months.

✳ **Meal Prep Tip:** This granola is great sprinkled over Greek yogurt, eaten as cereal with your favorite milk or non-dairy milk, or on its own as a crunchy treat.

✳ **Cooking Tip:** The granola will continue to crisp as it cools. You can let it cool right in the slow cooker or speed up the process by spreading it onto a baking sheet.

Per Serving: Calories: 223; Protein: 6g; Fat: 6g; Carbohydrates: 39g; Fiber: 4g; Sodium: 19mg

Apple-Cinnamon Steel Cut Oatmeal

Serves 6 / Prep Time: 5 minutes / Cook Time: 8 hours (Low)

5-INGREDIENT   FREEZER-FRIENDLY   ONE-POT   VEGAN

Steel cut oats are less processed than rolled oats, which makes them a healthy choice for breakfast. They have a slightly nutty flavor and a chewy texture that I love. They also take longer to cook, which means they're perfect for making in the slow cooker. Although it is possible to cook the oats directly in the slow cooker, cooking them in a baking dish surrounded by water will give you more consistent results and make them less prone to burning around the edges.

1½ cups steel cut oats

6 cups water

2 apples, shredded

⅓ cup pure maple syrup

1 tablespoon ground cinnamon

2 teaspoons vanilla extract

¼ teaspoon kosher salt

1. In an oven-safe baking dish small enough to fit in your slow cooker, stir together the oats, water, apples, maple syrup, cinnamon, vanilla, and salt until well mixed. Carefully place the dish inside your slow cooker. Pour a few cups of water into the slow cooker, around the dish—it should come about halfway up the sides of the dish.

2. Cover the slow cooker and cook on Low heat for 8 hours. Stir well.

3. Refrigerate individual portions in airtight containers for up to 5 days, or freeze for up to 3 months.

Meal Prep Tip: Start these oats before bed and have a warm, nutritious breakfast waiting when you wake up. You can also make this oatmeal ahead and reheat it in the microwave or on the stovetop. If it's too thick, thin it with a tablespoon or two of milk or water.

Substitution Tip: For a more decadent bowl of oats, substitute milk or nondairy milk for half the water in the oats.

Per Serving: Calories: 216; Protein: 6g; Fat: 3g; Carbohydrates: 46g; Fiber: 6g; Sodium: 99mg

Lemon-Blueberry Oatmeal

Serves 6 / Prep Time: 5 minutes / Cook Time: 8 hours (Low)

5-INGREDIENT   DAIRY-FREE   FREEZER-FRIENDLY   ONE-POT   VEGETARIAN

Cooking oatmeal in a slow cooker gives it an extra creamy texture that feels decadent. Oatmeal is usually thought of as a cold-weather breakfast, but brightening it with tart lemon and fresh blueberries gives it a fresh summer feel. Of course, swap in your favorite berries to make this recipe your own—try raspberries or chopped strawberries.

1½ cups old-fashioned rolled oats
4½ cups water
Grated zest of 2 lemons
Juice of 2 lemons
¼ teaspoon kosher salt
1 cup fresh blueberries
2 tablespoons honey (optional)

1. In an oven-safe baking dish small enough to fit in your slow cooker, stir together the oats, water, lemon zest, lemon juice, and salt. Carefully place the dish inside your slow cooker. Pour a few cups of water into the slow cooker, around the dish—it should come about halfway up the sides of the dish.

2. Cover the slow cooker and cook on Low heat for 8 hours.

3. Stir in the blueberries and honey (if using).

4. Refrigerate individual portions in airtight containers for up to 5 days, or freeze for up to 3 months.

⁎ **Meal Prep Tip:** Leftovers are great reheated in the microwave for a minute or two, or enjoyed straight from the refrigerator. If the oatmeal thickens too much after it sits, thin it with a splash of water or milk.

⁎ **Substitution Tip:** If fresh blueberries aren't in season, use frozen wild blueberries. They only take a few minutes to thaw in the hot cereal.

Per Serving: Calories: 94; Protein: 3g; Fat: 2g; Carbohydrates: 19g; Fiber: 3g; Sodium: 99mg

Shakshuka

Serves 6 / Prep Time: 10 minutes / Cook Time: 8 hours (Low)

FREEZER-FRIENDLY GLUTEN-FREE ONE-POT VEGETARIAN

Shakshuka is a popular dish across the Middle East and Northern Africa. In its simplest form, shakshuka is a warmly seasoned tomato sauce with eggs. In this version, I add eggplant for a boost of nutrition and flavor. I like to serve it with bread for sopping up every bit of sauce.

1 eggplant, peeled
  and chopped
2 (14.5-ounce) cans
  fire-roasted diced
  tomatoes, drained
1 onion, diced
1 red bell pepper, seeded
  and diced
2 garlic cloves, minced
2 teaspoons paprika
½ teaspoon ground cumin
¼ teaspoon
  cayenne pepper
6 large eggs
¼ cup crumbled feta
  cheese (optional)

1. In your slow cooker, stir together the egg-plant, tomatoes, onion, red bell pepper, garlic, paprika, cumin, and cayenne.

2. Cover the slow cooker and cook on Low heat for 8 hours. Mix well.

3. Crack the eggs into the sauce. Turn the slow cooker to High heat, re-cover it, and cook for 5 to 8 minutes for runny yolks, or up to 15 minutes for firmer yolks, if you prefer.

4. Sprinkle with feta to serve (if using).

5. Refrigerate individual portions, topped with feta, in airtight containers for up to 5 days, or freeze up to 4 months.

✳ **Prep Ahead:** Complete step 1, putting the ingredients in an airtight container. Measure the feta (if using) into a separate container. Refrigerate for up to 5 days, or freeze for up to 3 months. Throw the slow cooker ingredients in the slow cooker before bed, and there's no mess in the kitchen. Add the eggs as directed. If frozen, thaw the ingredients in the refrigerator overnight before adding to your slow cooker.

✳ **Cooking Tip:** To reheat, microwave on low power for 1 to 2 minutes, or heat in a pot on the stove over medium heat for 5 to 8 minutes.

Per Serving: Calories: 147; Protein: 9g; Fat: 5g; Carbohydrates: 17g; Fiber: 6g; Sodium: 472mg

Savory Quinoa Breakfast Bowls

Serves 6 / Prep Time: 10 minutes / Cook Time: 3 hours (High)

DAIRY-FREE FREEZER-FRIENDLY GLUTEN-FREE

These savory breakfast bowls are a riff on one of my favorite breakfast sandwiches, which features smoky chorizo and sweet roasted red peppers. In this recipe, nutty quinoa stands in for the bread. This bowl gets really good when you mix in the slightly runny egg yolk. I've included this recipe in the breakfast chapter, but these are great for dinner, too.

12 ounces chicken chorizo, crumbled

1½ cups quinoa, rinsed

3 cups Vegetable Broth (page 134), or low-sodium vegetable broth

2 red bell peppers, seeded and sliced

1 sweet onion, thinly sliced

6 large eggs

1. In a sauté pan over medium-high heat, cook the chorizo for 5 to 7 minutes, or until deeply browned. Transfer to your slow cooker. Add the quinoa, vegetable broth, red bell peppers, and onion.

2. Cover the slow cooker and cook on High heat for 3 hours, or until the quinoa is soft and the liquid is absorbed.

3. Crack the eggs into the slow cooker. Re-cover the cooker and cook for 5 to 8 minutes for runny yolks, or longer for firmer yolks, if you prefer.

4. Refrigerate individual portions in airtight containers for up to 4 days.

❋ **Meal Prep Tip:** Reheat in the microwave on low power for 1 minute, stirring halfway through the cooking time. If you want to freeze this recipe for later, cook the eggs as desired when ready to serve. The quinoa and chorizo base will keep well frozen in an airtight container for up to 2 months.

Per Serving: Calories: 369; Protein: 22g; Fat: 14g; Carbohydrates: 39g; Fiber: 5g; Sodium: 486mg

Sweet Potato and Sausage Breakfast Hash

Serves 6 / Prep Time: 10 minutes / Cook Time: 6 hours (Low); 3 hours (High)

DAIRY-FREE FREEZER-FRIENDLY GLUTEN-FREE ONE-POT

This dish was inspired by the breakfast skillets served at my favorite diner. Tossing the vegetables in olive oil helps them crisp a little, especially when placed around the edges of the slow cooker where the heat is most intense. The liquid released by the peppers and onions is enough to steam the sweet potatoes until they're perfectly tender.

6 sweet potatoes, diced

1 red onion, diced

2 bell peppers, any color, seeded and diced

2 tablespoons olive oil

4 garlic cloves, minced

1 tablespoon dried thyme

1 teaspoon paprika

1 teaspoon kosher salt

½ teaspoon freshly ground black pepper

12 turkey breakfast sausages

1. In your slow cooker, combine the sweet potatoes, red onion, and bell peppers. Drizzle in the oil and stir well so that everything is coated. Stir in the garlic, thyme, paprika, salt, and black pepper. Place the sausages on top of the vegetables.

2. Wrap the slow cooker lid with a clean kitchen towel to trap condensation and cover the slow cooker with it. Cook on Low heat for 6 hours, or High heat for 3 hours.

3. Refrigerate individual portions in airtight containers for up to 5 days, or freeze for up to 2 months.

+ **Meal Prep Tip:** Get creative with the ingredients. Sometimes I add diced zucchini or mushrooms. You can also stir in fresh baby spinach or Ratatouille (page 136). To reheat, microwave for 1 to 1½ minutes.

+ **Ingredient Tip:** Use any color bell pepper for this recipe. I like to use one green pepper and one yellow, orange, or red pepper.

Per Serving: Calories: 395; Protein: 19g; Fat: 19g; Carbohydrates: 40g; Fiber: 5g; Sodium:1,166mg

Butternut Squash, Sun-Dried Tomato, and Goat Cheese Frittata

Serves 6 / Prep Time: 5 minutes / Cook Time: 1½ to 2 hours (High)

FREEZER-FRIENDLY GLUTEN-FREE VEGETARIAN

Eggs don't usually freeze or reheat well, but frittatas and quiches are the exception, which makes them great for meal prep. For this recipe, I combined sweet butternut squash, savory sun-dried tomatoes, and tangy goat cheese to make a fluffy frittata that's perfect for grab and go. It's also great for brunch with a simple side salad dressed with oil, balsamic vinegar, and lots of freshly ground black pepper. If you can't find butternut squash, use sweet potato.

½ cup sun-dried tomatoes, chopped

Hot water, for soaking the tomatoes

12 large eggs

½ cup milk

¼ teaspoon kosher salt

½ teaspoon freshly ground black pepper

2 cups diced butternut squash

4 ounces soft goat cheese, crumbled

1. In a small bowl, combine the dried tomatoes with enough hot water to cover. Let sit for 5 minutes until soft. Drain.

2. In a large bowl, whisk the eggs and milk. Season with the salt and pepper. Stir in the squash and softened tomatoes. Pour the egg mixture into your slow cooker. Scatter the goat cheese over the top.

3. Wrap the slow cooker lid with a clean kitchen towel to trap condensation and cover the slow cooker with it. Cook on High heat for 1½ to 2 hours until set.

4. Refrigerate individual portions in airtight containers for 3 to 4 days, or freeze for up to 2 months wrapped in a double layer of plastic wrap and aluminum foil.

   ✳ **Meal Prep Tip:** To reheat, cover the frittata with a damp paper towel and microwave on low power for 1 to 2 minutes, or grab a piece straight from the refrigerator.

   ✳ **Ingredient Tip:** Look near the spices for dry-packed sun-dried tomatoes, which have less saturated fat and aren't as greasy as the jarred version.

Per Serving: Calories: 247; Protein: 18g; Fat: 15g; Carbohydrates: 12g; Fiber: 3g; Sodium: 416mg

Western Scrambled Eggs

Serves 6 / **Prep Time: 10 minutes** / **Cook Time: 2 hours (Low)**

5-INGREDIENT GLUTEN-FREE

My favorite scrambled eggs are cooked for a long time over super low heat, until they're creamy and almost custard-like. The slow cooker replicates that heat well, without the need to stand over the stove watching the eggs cook. Eggs have a tendency to stick, so be sure to spray the inside of your slow cooker generously with cooking spray, even if you use a liner.

1 tablespoon olive oil

2 green bell peppers, seeded and diced

1 shallot, minced

12 large eggs

1½ cups milk

½ teaspoon kosher salt

¼ teaspoon freshly ground black pepper

6 Canadian bacon slices, diced

Nonstick cooking spray

1. In a small skillet over medium heat. Add the green bell peppers and shallot. Cook for 3 to 4 minutes until softened.

2. In a large bowl, whisk the eggs and milk. Season with salt and black pepper. Stir in the Canadian bacon and cooked vegetables.

3. Generously coat your slow cooker with cooking spray. Pour in the egg mixture.

4. Cover the slow cooker and cook on Low heat for 1½ hours. Stir the eggs, re-cover the cooker, and cook for 30 minutes more.

5. Refrigerate individual portions in airtight containers for up to 3 days.

✛ **Meal Prep Tip:** These eggs are delicious on their own as a simple scramble, but you can switch things up by piling them on a whole-grain English muffin or wrapping them in a tortilla. To reheat, cover the eggs with a damp paper towel and microwave on low power for 1 to 2 minutes.

✛ **Substitution Tip:** Substitute 1 cup of chopped broccoli florets for the green bell peppers.

Per Serving: Calories: 258; Protein: 20g; Fat: 16g; Carbohydrates: 7g; Fiber: 1g; Sodium: 727mg

Sausage and Broccoli Frittata

Serves 6 / Prep Time: 10 minutes / Cook Time: 2½ hours (High)

5-INGREDIENT   FREEZER-FRIENDLY   GLUTEN-FREE

This frittata only has five ingredients, but the Italian sausage and broccoli give it tons of flavor. Use either hot or sweet sausage, depending on your mood. Placing a clean kitchen towel under your slow cooker lid traps the steam as it rises, so condensation doesn't drip back onto the eggs and make them soggy.

Nonstick cooking spray
1 pound ground
   Italian sausage
12 large eggs
1 cup milk
½ teaspoon sea salt
½ teaspoon freshly
   ground black pepper
1 shallot, minced
2 cups bite-size
   broccoli florets

1. Generously coat your slow cooker with cooking spray.

2. In a hot, dry skillet over medium-high heat, cook the sausage for 5 to 7 minutes, breaking it up with a spoon, until browned but not cooked through. Drain the fat.

3. In your slow cooker, whisk the eggs and milk to combine. Season with salt and pepper. Stir in the shallot, broccoli, and sausage.

4. Wrap the slow cooker lid with a clean kitchen towel to trap condensation and cover the slow cooker with it. Cook on High heat for 2½ hours, or until the center of the frittata is set and the edges are slightly browned.

5. Refrigerate individual portions in airtight containers for 3 to 4 days, or freeze for up to 2 months wrapped in a double layer of plastic wrap and aluminum foil.

✳ **Prep Ahead:** Instead of combining the ingredients directly in your slow cooker, place them in an airtight container and refrigerate overnight, or freeze for up to 2 months. If frozen, thaw the ingredients in the refrigerator overnight before adding to your slow cooker. To reheat the cooked frittata, cover it with a damp paper towel and microwave on low power for 1 to 2 minutes.

Per Serving: Calories: 373; Protein: 25g; Fat: 26g; Carbohydrates: 5g; Fiber: 1g; Sodium: 1,034mg

Hash Brown Breakfast Bake

Serves 6 / **Prep Time: 5 minutes** / **Cook Time: 8 hours (Low)**

FREEZER-FRIENDLY GLUTEN-FREE

I'm typically all about using fresh ingredients, but fresh potatoes just don't work in this recipe, so we will work with frozen hash browns instead. They work well because they are partially cooked, which removes some of the liquid and helps keep them firm. Look for all-natural hash browns that list potatoes as the only ingredient on the package.

1 pound breakfast sausage

1 pound frozen shredded hash brown potatoes, thawed

Nonstick cooking spray

1 onion, shredded

6 large eggs, beaten

2 cups plain fat-free Greek yogurt

1 teaspoon dry mustard

½ teaspoon kosher salt

½ teaspoon freshly ground black pepper

1. In a skillet over medium heat, crumble the sausage and cook for 6 to 8 minutes until browned and cooked through. Blot the hash browns dry with a towel to remove any excess water.

2. Coat your slow cooker with cooking spray and add the hash browns, onion, eggs, yogurt, dry mustard, salt, and pepper. Stir in the sausage.

3. Cover the slow cooker and cook on Low heat for 8 hours.

4. Refrigerate individual portions in airtight containers for up to 4 days, or freeze for up to 2 months.

⁜ **Prep Ahead:** Start this in the morning so that it's ready at night. Or, better yet, let it cook while you sleep and wake up to a freshly cooked breakfast. To reheat, microwave on low power for 30 seconds to 1 minute.

Per Serving: Calories: 454; Protein: 29g; Fat: 29g; Carbohydrates: 21g; Fiber: 1g; Sodium: 984mg

Tex-Mex Migas

Serves 6 / Prep Time: 10 minutes / Cook Time: 2 to 3 hours (Low)

GLUTEN-FREE   VEGETARIAN

The ingredients in migas can vary greatly depending on your location. In Spain, it's made with leftover bread, in Portugal it's often made with potatoes, and in Mexico it's made with day-old tortillas fried in oil. Rather than frying tortillas, I use tortilla chips combined with fresh salsa and black beans to make a hearty breakfast casserole. I like using organic corn tortilla chips in this recipe; for the best flavor, look for ones made with just corn, oil, and salt. Late July and Jackson's Honest are two good brands. You can also use grain-free tortilla chips made from cassava flour.

4 cups tortilla chips

8 large eggs

1½ cups fresh salsa

1 (15.5-ounce) can low-sodium black beans, drained and rinsed

1 red bell pepper, seeded and chopped

1 tablespoon ground cumin

1 cup shredded pepper Jack cheese

¼ cup milk

¼ cup fresh cilantro, chopped

2 teaspoons hot sauce

1. Layer the chips in your slow cooker.

2. In a large bowl, whisk the eggs, salsa, black beans, red bell pepper, cumin, cheese, and milk to combine. Pour the egg mixture over the chips.

3. Cover the slow cooker and cook on Low heat for 2 to 3 hours, or until set. Top with cilantro and hot sauce to serve.

4. Refrigerate individual portions in airtight containers for 3 to 4 days.

✳ **Meal Prep Tip:** This recipe is just as delicious for dinner as it is for breakfast. To reheat, microwave on low power for 45 seconds to 1 minute.

Per Serving: Calories: 452; Protein: 21g; Fat: 23g; Carbohydrates: 43g; Fiber: 8g; Sodium: 808mg

Cranberry-Orange Scones

Serves 6 / Prep Time: 10 minutes / Cook Time: 2½ hours (High)

FREEZER-FRIENDLY VEGETARIAN

I have a soft spot for scones, but they're traditionally made with lots of butter or cream, so they're not a great option for every day. This healthier scone recipe is based on a standard cream scone, swapping plain Greek yogurt for heavy cream and whole-wheat flour for all-purpose flour. Orange zest and dried cranberries provide tons of flavor.

2 cups white
  whole-wheat flour
¼ cup sugar
2 teaspoons
  baking powder
Grated zest of 1 orange
½ teaspoon kosher salt
1 cup plain fat-free
  Greek yogurt
¼ cup dried cranberries
Nonstick cooking spray

1. In a large bowl, combine the flour, sugar, baking powder, orange zest, and salt.

2. Slowly drizzle in the yogurt, stirring to form a thick dough. Stir in the cranberries. Form the dough into a disk, about ¾ inch thick.

3. Coat your slow cooker with cooking spray. Transfer the dough to the prepared slow cooker. Using a butter knife, gently cut the dough into 8 triangles.

4. Cover the slow cooker and cook on High heat for 2½ hours. Let cool completely.

5. Store individual portions in airtight containers at room temperature for up to 5 days, or freeze for up to 3 months wrapped in a double layer of plastic wrap and aluminum foil.

✳ **Prep Ahead:** These scones cook for only 2½ hours, but they're best when fully cooled. Turn off the "keep warm" feature of your slow cooker and put them in to bake before you go to bed. You'll wake up to perfect scones!

✳ **Substitution Tip:** Substitute ½ teaspoon orange extract for the zest, if you prefer. If you don't like orange, use vanilla extract.

Per Serving: Calories: 204; Protein: 9g; Fat: 1g; Carbohydrates: 39g; Fiber: 5g; Sodium: 372mg

Pumpkin Cinnamon Rolls

Serves 8 / Prep Time: 15 minutes / Cook Time: 1½ to 2 hours (High)

DAIRY-FREE FREEZER-FRIENDLY VEGETARIAN

Who doesn't love a soft, sweet cinnamon roll? These rolls are swirled with pumpkin instead of the traditional butter filling, which cuts down on saturated fat and adds flavor and vitamin A. Cinnamon and sugar add the perfect amount of sweetness and give these rolls a pumpkin pie vibe that's perfect for fall. These rolls are made with whole-wheat flour, so they'll have a rustic texture and slightly nutty flavor.

2½ cups white whole-wheat flour, plus more for the work surface

1 teaspoon salt

¾ cup warm water

1 (0.25-ounce) packet quick-rise yeast, or instant dry yeast

¼ cup honey

1 tablespoon olive oil

2 teaspoons vanilla extract

1 cup pumpkin puree

2 tablespoons sugar

2 tablespoons ground cinnamon

1. In a large bowl, combine the flour and salt.

2. In a small bowl, whisk the warm water, yeast, and honey to combine. Stir in the oil and vanilla.

3. Slowly stir the yeast mixture into the flour mixture to create a soft dough.

4. Dust a work surface with flour and turn the dough out onto it. Knead for 5 minutes until smooth and elastic. Roll the dough into a large rectangle, about 7 by 10 inches.

5. Spread the pumpkin over the dough. Sprinkle with sugar and cinnamon. Working from the long edge, roll the dough into a log. Cut the log crosswise into 8 rolls and place the rolls in your slow cooker.

6. Cover the slow cooker and cook on High heat for 1½ to 2 hours, or until cooked through (they should reach an internal temperature of 190°F). Let cool.

7. Store the cinnamon rolls in an airtight container for up to 1 week, or freeze for up to 3 months wrapped in a double layer of plastic wrap and aluminum foil.

- **Meal Prep Tip:** Using instant yeast means these cinnamon rolls don't need to rise before you bake them, which makes prep even faster. Serve at room temperature, or reheat by wrapping in a paper towel and microwaving on low power for 30 seconds.
- **Substitution Tip:** Swap apple butter or your favorite all-fruit spread for the pumpkin—I like raspberry—for a different spin on these rolls. For softer rolls with a milder flavor, use half white whole-wheat flour and half all-purpose flour.

Per Serving: Calories: 202; Protein: 6g; Fat: 3g; Carbohydrates: 38g; Fiber: 6g; Sodium: 293mg

Banana Bread

Serves 6 / Prep Time: 10 minutes / Cook Time: 2 hours (High)

FREEZER-FRIENDLY VEGETARIAN

Make banana bread year-round without heating up your house. The slow cooker gives this bread a great texture, with crispy edges and a moist center. It has a subtle nutty flavor from the whole-wheat flour and isn't too sweet, so it's perfect for breakfast.

1 cup white
  whole-wheat flour

2 teaspoons
  baking powder

¼ teaspoon kosher salt

3 very ripe bananas

¼ cup milk

¼ cup coconut sugar,
  or honey

2 large eggs

1 teaspoon vanilla extract

Butter, or nonstick
  cooking spray,
  for preparing the
  slow cooker

¼ cup dark
  chocolate chips

1. In a large bowl, whisk the flour, baking powder, and salt to combine.

2. In a medium bowl, mash the bananas. Whisk in the milk, coconut sugar, eggs, and vanilla until blended. Gently stir the wet ingredients into the dry ingredients. Don't mix them more than you need to get everything incorporated.

3. Coat your slow cooker with butter and pour in the batter. Sprinkle the chocolate chips over the top.

4. Cover the slow cooker and cook on High heat for 2 hours, or until the bread is cooked through and a toothpick inserted into the center comes out clean. The temperature in the center of the bread should be 200°F. Let cool completely, then coax the bread onto a plate.

5. Refrigerate individual portions in airtight containers for up to 5 days, or freeze for up to 3 months wrapped in a double layer of plastic wrap and aluminum foil.

* **Meal Prep Tip:** For a treat, spread 1 tablespoon of your favorite nut butter onto a slice of this bread.
* **Substitution Tip:** If you prefer a sweeter taste, use semi-sweet chocolate chips; if you like things less sweet, cut the sugar and use chopped nuts instead of the chocolate chips.

Per Serving: Calories: 231; Protein: 6g; Fat: 6g; Carbohydrates: 41g; Fiber: 4g; Sodium: 292mg

CHAPTER 3

Soups, Stews, and Chilis

White Bean Soup with Pesto

Serves 6 / Prep Time: 10 minutes / Cook Time: 8 hours (Low); 3 hours (High)

FREEZER-FRIENDLY GLUTEN-FREE VEGETARIAN

This white bean soup is shockingly flavorful given how simple the recipe is. Don't be tempted to skip the bay leaves, which add an herbal, slightly floral taste that really makes this recipe extra special. Pesto swirled into each portion adds even more herby flavor. I've included a quick recipe for homemade pesto, but you can also use fresh pesto from the produce section of your favorite grocery store.

For the pesto

¼ cup fresh basil leaves

2 garlic cloves, peeled

1 ounce Parmesan cheese, finely grated

1 tablespoon olive oil

For the white bean soup

3 cups Vegetable Broth (page 134), or low-sodium vegetable broth

3 (15.5-ounce) cans low-sodium navy beans, drained and rinsed

2 leeks, washed well, white and light green parts thinly sliced

4 garlic cloves, minced

3 bay leaves

¼ teaspoon freshly ground black pepper

To make the pesto

1. On a cutting board, combine the basil, garlic, and Parmesan cheese. Using a large, sharp knife, finely mince the ingredients together. Transfer to a small bowl and stir in the oil until smooth. Set aside.

To make the white bean soup

2. In your slow cooker, stir together the vegetable broth, navy beans, leeks, garlic, bay leaves, and pepper.

3. Cover the slow cooker and cook on Low heat for 8 hours, or High heat for 3 hours.

4. Remove and discard the bay leaves. Using an immersion blender, blend the soup into a thin puree.

5. Refrigerate individual portions of the soup in airtight containers, each topped with 1 teaspoon of pesto, for up to 5 days, or freeze for up to 3 months.

* **Prep Ahead:** Combine the soup ingredients in an airtight container. Portion the pesto into a second container—a small jar or plastic bag works well. Refrigerate for up to 5 days, or freeze for 3 months. If frozen, thaw the ingredients in the refrigerator overnight before adding to your slow cooker.

* **Substitution Tip:** For a meat-eaters' soup, add 6 ounces of pancetta, diced, along with the rest of the ingredients in step 1.

Per Serving: Calories: 236; Protein: 14g; Fat: 3g; Carbohydrates: 39g; Fiber: 13g; Sodium: 505mg

Triple Onion Soup

Serves 6 / Prep Time: 15 minutes / Cook Time: 8 to 10 hours (Low) plus 30 minutes (High)

FREEZER-FRIENDLY GLUTEN-FREE ONE-POT

The low, steady heat of slow cookers makes them perfect for caramelizing onions. It's almost like magic. The ingredients will look very dry at first, but don't be tempted to add more liquid—the onions will release a significant amount of water as they cook. Once the onions are caramelized, all it takes is a little broth and some fresh thyme to turn them into a deeply flavorful soup.

3 yellow onions,
   thinly sliced
2 shallots, thinly sliced
1 leek, washed well, white
   and light green parts
   thinly sliced
1 tablespoon butter
2 cups Beef Bone
   Broth (page 133), or
   low-sodium beef broth
1 teaspoon fresh
   thyme leaves

1. In your slow cooker, combine the onions, shallots, leek, and butter.

2. Cover the slow cooker and cook on Low heat for 8 to 10 hours, until deeply caramelized and fragrant.

3. Stir in the beef broth and thyme. Re-cover the cooker and cook on High heat for 30 minutes until heated through.

4. Refrigerate individual portions in airtight containers for up to 5 days, or freeze for up to 3 months.

* **Prep Ahead:** Store the sliced onions, shallots, leek, and butter in a medium airtight container. Place the broth and thyme in a second container. Refrigerate both for up to 5 days. I like using a Mason jar for the broth so it can be poured into the slow cooker easily.

* **Ingredient Tip:** Leeks are grown in sandy soil, so it's important to wash them well to remove any grit. Halve the leeks lengthwise, then thinly cut the halves into half-moons. Rinse thoroughly in plenty of water and drain well.

Per Serving: Calories: 57; Protein: 2g; Fat: 2g; Carbohydrates: 8g; Fiber: 1g; Sodium: 169mg

Broccoli Cheddar Soup

Serves 6 / **Prep Time: 5 minutes** / **Cook Time: 8 hours (Low)**

5-INGREDIENT FREEZER-FRIENDLY GLUTEN-FREE ONE-POT

I don't know many people who don't go googly-eyed over a steamy bowl of broccoli Cheddar soup. There's just something so comforting about that classic pairing. Many recipes call for thickening the broth with flour or cream, but I prefer to use more broccoli and gently blend the soup before serving. That way, you'll get a cleaner, more vibrant broccoli flavor.

8 cups broccoli florets
5 carrots, shredded
¼ cup minced shallot
3 cups Chicken
   Stock (page 132),
   or low-sodium
   chicken broth
1 cup shredded
   Cheddar cheese
¼ teaspoon sea salt

1. In your slow cooker, combine the broccoli, carrots, shallot, and chicken stock.

2. Cover the slow cooker and cook on Low heat for 8 hours.

3. If desired, using an immersion blender, lightly blend the soup, leaving some texture.

4. Stir in the cheese. Re-cover the cooker and let sit for 5 to 10 minutes until the cheese is thoroughly melted. Season with salt.

5. Refrigerate individual portions in airtight containers for up to 4 days, or freeze for up to 3 months.

* **Prep Ahead:** Combine the broccoli, carrots, shallot, broth, and salt in an airtight container and place the cheese in a separate container. Refrigerate for up to 4 days, or freeze for up to 3 months. If frozen, thaw the ingredients overnight in the refrigerator before adding to your slow cooker.

* **Ingredient Tip:** I buy bricks of cheese and shred them myself. Pre-shredded cheese is often coated in starch, which prevents it from melting well.

Per Serving: Calories: 147; Protein: 7g; Fat: 6g; Carbohydrates: 12g; Fiber: 4g; Sodium: 314mg

Mexican Street Corn Soup

Serves 6 / Prep Time: 10 minutes / Cook Time: 8 hours (Low)

FREEZER-FRIENDLY GLUTEN-FREE ONE-POT VEGETARIAN

This creamy soup was inspired by one served at my favorite Mexican restaurant. The sweetness of corn pairs so well with a touch of heat, acid, and cream that it truly hits every flavor note. This soup has a good kick to it, so adjust the amount of chili powder based on how spicy you like things. One teaspoon is a good starting point.

1 pound frozen corn kernels, thawed

1 russet potato, peeled and diced

1 poblano pepper, minced

½ red onion, minced

2 cups Vegetable Broth (page 134), or low-sodium vegetable broth

1 teaspoon ancho chili powder

½ teaspoon kosher salt

2 tablespoons plain fat-free Greek yogurt

¼ cup fresh cilantro, chopped

Juice of 1 lime (optional)

1. In your slow cooker, combine the corn, potato, poblano, red onion, vegetable broth, chili powder, and salt.

2. Cover the slow cooker and cook on Low heat for 8 hours.

3. Using an immersion blender, gently blend the soup, keeping some texture.

4. Stir in the yogurt.

5. Refrigerate individual portions in airtight containers, each topped with a sprinkle of cilantro and lime juice (if using), for up to 5 days, or freeze for up to 3 months.

⁜ **Prep Ahead:** Combine the corn, potato, poblano, onion, broth, chili powder, and salt in an airtight container, making sure the potatoes are completely submerged. Measure the yogurt and cilantro into separate containers. Refrigerate for up to 4 days.

⁜ **Substitution Tip:** For a more traditional flavor, use sour cream in place of yogurt.

Per Serving: Calories: 98; Protein: 3g; Fat: 1g; Carbohydrates: 22g; Fiber: 3g; Sodium: 213mg

Butternut Squash and Apple Bisque

Serves 6 / Prep Time: 10 minutes / Cook Time: 8 hours (Low); 3 hours (High)

DAIRY-FREE FREEZER-FRIENDLY GLUTEN-FREE ONE-POT

Apples and a drizzle of pure maple syrup add a subtle sweetness to this creamy butternut squash soup, and a sprinkle of red pepper flakes keeps it from being too cloying. This is the perfect soup for a chilly fall or winter night. A bowl of it is delicious on its own but, when I'm feeling extra ambitious, it's also fantastic with a grilled cheese sandwich.

3 pounds butternut squash, peeled and diced

2 apples, peeled, cored, and diced

1 leek, washed well, white and light green parts thinly sliced

2 cups Chicken Stock (page 132), or low-sodium chicken broth

½ teaspoon kosher salt

½ teaspoon red pepper flakes

1 cup canned coconut milk

6 tablespoons pure maple syrup

1. In your slow cooker, combine the squash, apples, leek, chicken stock, salt, and red pepper flakes.

2. Cover the slow cooker and cook on Low heat for 8 hours, or High heat for 3 hours.

3. Using an immersion blender, blend the soup into a smooth puree. Stir in the coconut milk and maple syrup.

4. Refrigerate individual portions in airtight containers for up to 4 days, or freeze for up to 3 months.

✳ **Prep Ahead:** Combine the diced squash, apples, leek, chicken stock, salt, and red pepper flakes in an airtight container. Combine the coconut milk and maple syrup in a small jar. (I love saving empty condiment jars to repurpose for things like this.) Refrigerate for up to 4 days.

✳ **Ingredient Tip:** Use pure maple syrup, not pancake syrup, which is just flavored corn syrup.

Per Serving: Calories: 224; Protein: 4g; Fat: 8g; Carbohydrates: 36g; Fiber: 5g; Sodium: 232mg

Samosa Soup

Serves 6 / **Prep Time: 10 minutes** / **Cook Time: 8 hours (Low); 2 hours (High)**

FREEZER-FRIENDLY GLUTEN-FREE ONE-POT VEGETARIAN

This twist on potato soup is inspired by the flavor of samosas, fried pastries filled with potatoes, peas, and spices that are popular Indian street fare. Jalapeño peppers add flavor, but the heat mellows significantly due to the long cooking time. If you want your soup to have more of a kick, add two peppers.

6 russet potatoes, chopped

4 cups Vegetable Broth (page 134), or low-sodium vegetable broth

2 shallots, minced

1 jalapeño pepper, minced

1 (12-ounce) can fat-free evaporated milk

1 teaspoon ground cumin

½ teaspoon kosher salt

¼ teaspoon ground turmeric

1 cup peas

2 tablespoons chopped fresh cilantro

1. In your slow cooker, combine the potatoes, vegetable broth, shallots, jalapeño, evaporated milk, cumin, salt, and turmeric.

2. Cover the slow cooker and cook on Low heat for 8 hours, or High heat for 2 hours.

3. Using an immersion blender, blend the soup into a slightly chunky puree. Stir in the peas and cilantro.

4. Refrigerate individual portions in airtight containers for up to 4 days, or freeze for up to 3 months.

* **Prep Ahead:** Combine the potatoes, shallots, jalapeño, cumin, salt, and turmeric in an airtight container. Add the broth, making sure the potatoes are completely submerged—this will help keep them from turning brown. Store the evaporated milk and peas in separate containers. Refrigerate for up to 2 days.

* **Cooking Tip:** If you don't have an immersion blender, use a potato masher or a heavy wooden spoon to blend the soup. A traditional blender can make the potatoes gummy.

Per Serving: Calories: 253; Protein: 11g; Fat: <1g; Carbohydrates: 53g; Fiber: 5g; Sodium: 303mg

Split Pea Soup

Serves 8 / Prep Time: 10 minutes / Cook Time: 8 hours (Low); 4 hours (High)

DAIRY-FREE   FREEZER-FRIENDLY   GLUTEN-FREE   ONE-POT

Split pea soup isn't the prettiest dish—the pale green color and porridge-like texture leave something to be desired—but it's delicious. It might actually be one of my favorite slow cooker recipes. Traditionally, a smoked ham hock is used to add a sweet and smoky layer. I prefer using diced pancetta, which adds a delicate floral flavor without a ton of smokiness.

12 ounces dried green split peas, rinsed well and picked over for any small stones or debris

8 cups Chicken Stock (page 132), or low-sodium chicken broth

4 carrots, diced

4 celery stalks, thinly sliced

1 onion, chopped

4 ounces pancetta, diced

1 tablespoon peppercorns

1. In your slow cooker, combine the split peas, chicken stock, carrots, celery, onion, pancetta, and peppercorns.

2. Cover the slow cooker and cook on Low heat for 8 hours, or High heat for 4 hours. Stir well to combine.

3. Refrigerate individual portions in airtight containers for up to 5 days, or freeze for up to 3 months.

✳ **Prep Ahead:** Rinse the split peas well and pick out and discard any small stones or other debris that might have found their way into the bag. Drain the peas and add them to an airtight container with the remaining ingredients. Refrigerate for up to 3 days.

✳ **Cooking Tip:** This soup is thick to begin with, but it thickens more as it sits. Add ½ to 1 cup of water to each serving to thin when reheating.

Per Serving: Calories: 230; Protein: 20g; Fat: 6g; Carbohydrates: 31g; Fiber: 12g; Sodium: 386mg

Moroccan-Spiced Lentil Soup

Serves 8 / **Prep Time: 10 minutes** / **Cook Time: 8 hours (Low)**

DAIRY-FREE FREEZER-FRIENDLY GLUTEN-FREE

Lentil soup is often overlooked, but I adore it. Lentils have a hearty flavor and starchy texture that make them a great option for stick-to-your-ribs meals. In this soup, I combine them with warm Moroccan-inspired spices and eggplant, which melts into the soup as it cooks and gives it a slightly creamy texture.

2 tablespoons olive oil

1 onion, diced

4 garlic cloves, minced

2 teaspoons ground cumin

1 teaspoon ground allspice

1 teaspoon ground cinnamon

½ teaspoon red pepper flakes

8 cups Chicken Stock (page 132), or low-sodium chicken broth

1½ cups dried brown lentils

1 small eggplant, peeled and diced

2 carrots, shredded

1 green bell pepper, seeded and diced

1. In a skillet over medium heat, heat the oil. Add the onion and cook for 3 to 4 minutes until translucent. Add the garlic, cumin, allspice, cinnamon, and red pepper flakes. Cook for 1 to 2 minutes, stirring constantly, until toasty and fragrant. Transfer the onion mixture to your slow cooker.

2. Stir in the chicken stock, lentils, eggplant, carrots, and green bell pepper.

3. Cover the slow cooker and cook on Low heat for 8 hours, or until the lentils are tender.

4. Refrigerate individual portions in airtight containers for up to 5 days, or freeze for up to 3 months.

＊ **Prep Ahead:** Sauté the onion and spices as instructed in step 1, then transfer to an airtight container. Add the broth, eggplant, carrots, and green bell pepper. Store the lentils in a separate container. Refrigerate for up to 4 days.

Per Serving: Calories: 189; Protein: 11g; Fat: 5g; Carbohydrates: 28g; Fiber: 12g; Sodium: 588mg

Vegetarian 3-Bean Chili

Serves 8 / Prep Time: 10 minutes / Cook Time: 8 hours (Low); 4 hours (High)

FREEZER-FRIENDLY ONE-POT VEGAN OPTION

When I was in seventh grade, we had a cooking unit during which we were tasked with making chili. Someone in the class was a vegetarian, and I volunteered to partner with them because no one else wanted to. Our chili was the best in the class, and this easy recipe is one of my favorites to this day.

1 (15.5-ounce) can
low-sodium pinto beans,
drained and rinsed well

1 (15.5-ounce) can
low-sodium black beans,
drained and rinsed well

1 (15.5-ounce) can
low-sodium kidney
beans, drained and
rinsed well

1 (15.5-ounce) can
fire-roasted tomatoes
with green chilies

1 onion, chopped

1 red bell pepper, seeded
and chopped

1 cup frozen corn

1 (1.25-ounce) packet
reduced-sodium chili
seasoning

Chives (optional)

Sour cream (optional)

Cheddar cheese,
shredded (optional)

1. In your slow cooker, combine the pinto, black, and kidney beans. Stir in the tomatoes and green chilies, onion, red bell pepper, corn and chili seasoning.

2. Cover the slow cooker and cook on Low heat for 8 hours, or High heat for 4 hours.

3. Refrigerate individual portions in airtight containers for up to 5 days, or freeze for up to 3 months. If preferred, serve topped with chives, sour cream, or cheese.

✴ **Prep Ahead:** Rinse and drain the beans, then add them to an airtight container with the remaining ingredients. Stir well to distribute the chili seasoning. Refrigerate for up to 5 days.

Per Serving: Calories: 202; Protein: 11g; Fat: 2g; Carbohydrates: 37g; Fiber: 12g; Sodium: 511mg

Chicken and Wild Rice Soup

Serves 8 / Prep Time: 15 minutes / Cook Time: 8 hours (Low); 4 hours (High)

FREEZER-FRIENDLY

Is there anything more comforting than creamy chicken and rice soup? This recipe might taste indulgent, but wild rice has fewer calories and more protein and fiber than brown rice—along with tons of flavor. Its chewy outer shell also means it takes longer to cook, making it perfect for slow cooker recipes.

2 tablespoons butter

3 carrots, halved and cut into coins

3 celery stalks, sliced

1 yellow onion, diced

1 teaspoon dried thyme

1 teaspoon garlic, minced

¼ cup all-purpose flour

8 cups Chicken Stock (page 132), or low-sodium chicken broth

1 cup wild rice

1 teaspoon salt

½ teaspoon freshly ground black pepper

1½ pounds boneless, skinless chicken breasts

¼ cup fresh parsley, chopped

1. In a skillet over medium heat, melt the butter. Add the carrots, celery, onion, and thyme. Cook for 5 minutes, stirring occasionally, until softened. Stir in the garlic.

2. Sprinkle the flour over the vegetables. Cook, stirring, for 3 minutes until the flour is no longer white. Transfer the vegetables to your slow cooker.

3. Pour in the chicken stock. Stir in the wild rice, salt, and pepper. Add the chicken breasts.

4. Cover the slow cooker and cook on Low heat for 8 hours, or High heat for 4 hours. Transfer the chicken to a cutting board and shred it, then return it to the soup. Stir in the parsley.

5. Refrigerate individual portions in airtight containers for up to 5 days, or freeze for up to 4 months.

* **Prep Ahead:** Sauté the vegetables as instructed in steps 1 and 2. Let cool, then transfer to an airtight container and add the broth, salt, and pepper. Store the rice and chicken each in a separate container. Refrigerate for up to 3 days.

* **Substitution Tip:** Use long-grain brown rice instead of wild rice. Or omit the rice completely and add 2 to 3 cups of cauliflower rice along with the parsley in step 4.

Per Serving: Calories: 239; Protein: 23g; Fat: 5g; Carbohydrates: 26g; Fiber: 2g; Sodium: 1,128mg

Easy Chicken Tortilla Soup

Serves 6 / Prep Time: 10 minutes / Cook Time: 8 hours (Low); 3 hours (High)

DAIRY-FREE FREEZER-FRIENDLY GLUTEN-FREE ONE-POT

This soup may be simple, but it's full of flavor. Using salsa instead of chopping bell peppers, onion, tomatoes, and garlic is a fantastic shortcut. Choose hot, medium, or mild salsa, depending on your preference. For the best flavor, look for fresh salsa sold in the produce section—it often has fewer preservatives and other add-ins compared to shelf-stable versions. For extra texture and crunch, I top the soup with tortilla chips. (Jackson's Honest is one of my favorite healthier brands.)

1 pound boneless, skinless chicken thighs

2 (15.5-ounce) cans low-sodium black beans, drained and rinsed

4½ cups Chicken Stock (page 132), or low-sodium chicken broth

3 cups fresh salsa

1½ cups corn

2 corn tortillas, cut into small pieces

1 tablespoon chili powder

¼ cup fresh cilantro, chopped

Juice of 1 lime

6 ounces corn tortilla chips (optional)

1. In your slow cooker, combine the chicken, black beans, chicken stock, salsa, corn, tortillas, and chili powder.

2. Cover the slow cooker and cook on Low heat for 8 hours, or High heat for 3 hours.

3. Transfer the chicken thighs to a cutting board and shred them, then return the chicken to the soup. Stir in the cilantro and lime juice.

4. Refrigerate individual portions in airtight containers for up to 5 days, or freeze for up to 4 months. When serving, top with the tortilla chips (if using).

✳ **Prep Ahead:** Combine the beans, chicken stock, salsa, corn, tortillas, and chili powder in an airtight container and refrigerate for up to 5 days. Refrigerate the chicken separately. Alternatively, add the chicken to the stock mixture and freeze for up to 3 months. If frozen, thaw the ingredients overnight in the refrigerator before adding to your slow cooker.

Per Serving: Calories: 321; Protein: 24g; Fat: 7g; Carbohydrates: 43g; Fiber: 12g; Sodium: 887mg

West African–Inspired Peanut Butter Stew

Serves 6 / Prep Time: 15 minutes / Cook Time: 10 hours (Low); 4 hours (High)

DAIRY-FREE   FREEZER-FRIENDLY   GLUTEN-FREE

I was introduced to peanut butter stew years ago by a coworker from Sierra Leone and I was immediately smitten. Peanut butter adds a unique layer of flavor to this stew that works beautifully. This stew is traditionally quite spicy, but I've really toned down this recipe. If you like more heat, habanero hot sauce added to your individual portion is a nice touch.

1 tablespoon olive oil

1 onion, sliced

4 garlic cloves, minced

1 tablespoon grated peeled fresh ginger

1½ pounds boneless, skinless chicken thighs, diced

2 sweet potatoes, peeled and cubed

1 jalapeño pepper, minced

1 (28-ounce) can crushed tomatoes in puree

½ cup natural peanut butter

1 cup Chicken Stock (page 132), or low-sodium chicken broth

Juice of 1 lime

Fresh cilantro, for garnish

1. In a skillet over medium heat, heat the oil. Add the onion and cook for 4 to 5 minutes until softened and translucent. Add the garlic and ginger and cook for 1 to 2 minutes more until fragrant. Transfer the cooked aromatics to your slow cooker.

2. Stir in the chicken, sweet potatoes, jalapeño, tomatoes, peanut butter, and chicken stock.

3. Cover the slow cooker and cook on Low heat for 10 hours, or High heat for 4 hours. Stir in the lime juice and garnish with cilantro.

4. Refrigerate individual portions in airtight containers for up to 5 days, or freeze for up to 3 months.

⊹ **Prep Ahead:** Sauté the aromatics as instructed in step 1. Let cool. Transfer to an airtight container and add the ingredients as indicated in step 2. Refrigerate for up to 2 days before finishing the recipe as directed.

⊹ **Substitution Tip:** I love the rich flavor and juicy texture of chicken thighs; if you prefer boneless, skinless chicken breasts, they work just as well.

Per Serving: Calories: 360; Protein: 28g; Fat: 21g; Carbohydrates: 21g; Fiber: 5g; Sodium: 427mg

Chicken Chili Verde

Serves 6 / Prep Time: 10 minutes / Cook Time: 6 hours (Low); 3 hours (High)

DAIRY-FREE FREEZER-FRIENDLY GLUTEN-FREE

Chili verde is a New Mexican staple with a flavorful sauce made from tomatillos and chile peppers. In this recipe, you'll use tomatillo salsa as a shortcut to making your own sauce. I'm partial to Frontera brand salsa, which has a bright, tangy flavor and a thin, sauce-like texture. Traditionally this chili is prepared without beans, but I can't resist adding some pintos to the pot to add fiber and break up the heaviness of all that meat.

12 ounces salsa verde

6 garlic cloves, minced

2 teaspoons
   ground cumin

2 teaspoons dried oregano

¼ teaspoon salt

¾ cup Chicken
   Stock (page 132),
   or low-sodium
   chicken broth

1½ cups canned
   low-sodium pinto beans,
   drained and rinsed

2 pounds boneless,
   skinless chicken breast

1. In your slow cooker, stir together the salsa, garlic, cumin, oregano, salt, chicken stock, and pinto beans.

2. Add the chicken.

3. Cover the slow cooker and cook on Low heat for 6 hours, or High heat for 3 hours.

4. Transfer the chicken to a cutting board and shred it, then return it to the pot.

5. Refrigerate individual portions in airtight containers for up to 5 days, or freeze for up to 3 months.

✳ **Prep Ahead:** Combine the ingredients as directed in step 1 in an airtight container and refrigerate for up to 5 days. Store the chicken in a separate container for up to 2 days, or keep it in the original unopened packaging until the best by date on the package.

✳ **Ingredient Tip:** Instead of chicken breasts, try boneless, skinless thighs. If you use thighs, this dish can be cooked for 8 hours without drying out the meat.

Per Serving: Calories: 217; Protein: 34g; Fat: 4g; Carbohydrates: 13g; Fiber: 4g; Sodium: 615mg

Zuppa Toscana

Serves 6 / Prep Time: 10 minutes / Cook Time: 8 hours (Low); 4 hours (High)

FREEZER-FRIENDLY GLUTEN-FREE

I always thought this soup was made up by American chain restaurants—so imagine my surprise when I saw it on menus across Tuscany. As it turns out, it's a classic Italian soup made with kale, beans, potatoes, bacon, and a tomato-based broth. It's delicious, but I prefer the creamy sausage soup I'm used to.

12 ounces hot Italian turkey sausage, crumbled
1 onion, diced
4 garlic cloves, minced
4 yellow potatoes, diced
6 cups Chicken Stock (page 132), or low-sodium chicken broth
½ teaspoon salt
½ teaspoon red pepper flakes
2 cups fat-free evaporated milk
1 bunch kale, chopped

1. In a skillet over medium-high heat, cook the sausage for 5 to 7 minutes until browned. Transfer the sausage to your slow cooker, leaving any grease in the skillet.

2. Turn the heat to medium and add the onion and garlic to the skillet. Cook for 5 minutes until softened but not browned. Transfer the vegetables to your slow cooker.

3. Stir in the potatoes, chicken stock, salt, red pepper flakes, and evaporated milk.

4. Cover the slow cooker and cook on Low heat for 8 hours, or High heat for 4 hours.

5. Stir in the kale until wilted.

6. Refrigerate individual portions in airtight containers for up to 5 days, or freeze for up to 3 months.

✴ **Prep Ahead:** Prepare the ingredients as instructed in steps 1 through 3, adding them to an airtight container. Chop the kale and store it separately. Refrigerate for up to 2 days.

✴ **Ingredient Tip:** Regular milk or cream can separate or curdle when cooked for a long time, so most recipes call for adding it just before serving. Evaporated milk is more stable, so you can add it at the beginning with the rest of the ingredients.

Per Serving: Calories: 277; Protein: 21g; Fat: 6g; Carbohydrates: 36g; Fiber: 3g; Sodium: 740mg

Beef and Bean Chili

Serves 8 / Prep Time: 15 minutes / Cook Time: 8 hours (Low); 3 hours (High)

DAIRY-FREE   FREEZER-FRIENDLY   GLUTEN-FREE

Chili is usually the first thing people make when they get a slow cooker, so this book wouldn't be complete without a chili recipe. Lean beef ensures your chili isn't too greasy, but if you go too lean it can be dry and not flavorful. For me, 90 percent lean is the sweet spot that balances the two.

1 tablespoon olive oil

1 onion, minced

2 garlic cloves, minced

2 pounds 90 percent lean ground beef

3 tablespoons chili powder

2 tablespoons ground cumin

1 teaspoon kosher salt

¼ teaspoon cayenne pepper (optional)

1 (29-ounce) can low-sodium dark red kidney beans, drained

1 (28-ounce) can fire-roasted crushed tomatoes

1 (4.5-ounce) can chopped green chilies

1. In a large skillet over medium heat, heat the oil. Add the onion and cook for 3 minutes until softened. Add the garlic and cook for 1 minute more.

2. Add the ground beef and cook, stirring to break up the meat, for 7 to 8 minutes until browned and cooked through. Stir in the chili powder, cumin, salt, and cayenne. Transfer the mixture to your slow cooker.

3. Stir in the kidney beans, tomatoes, and green chilies.

4. Cover the slow cooker and cook on Low heat for 8 hours, or High heat for 3 hours.

5. Refrigerate individual portions in airtight containers for up to 5 days, or freeze for up to 3 months.

✳ **Prep Ahead:** Prepare the chili through step 3, adding the ingredients to an airtight container. Refrigerate for up to 2 days, or freeze for up to 4 months. If frozen, thaw the ingredients overnight in the refrigerator before adding to your slow cooker.

✳ **Cooking Tip:** Sautéing the onion and garlic and browning the beef give the chili a more complex flavor. If you're pressed for time, skip these steps and add the raw ingredients directly to the slow cooker.

Per Serving: Calories: 312; Protein: 29g; Fat: 13g; Carbohydrates: 22g; Fiber: 7g; Sodium: 899mg

Classic Beef Stew

Serves 6 / Prep Time: 15 minutes / Cook Time: 8 hours (Low); 4 hours (High)

DAIRY-FREE FREEZER-FRIENDLY

Slow cookers are perfect for simmering beef over low heat for hours. Toasting flour in the same pan as the beef gives the stew a rich, nutty flavor and helps thicken the gravy. Be sure to scrape up as many of the browned bits from the pan as you can.

2 tablespoons olive oil

1½ pounds stew beef, trimmed and cubed

½ teaspoon freshly ground black pepper, plus more for seasoning

2 tablespoons white whole-wheat flour

1 cup Beef Bone Broth (page 133), or low-sodium beef broth

12 ounces yellow potatoes

6 carrots, cut into coins

1 onion, cut into 6 wedges

1 tablespoon tomato paste

2 teaspoons Italian seasoning

1 teaspoon Worcestershire sauce

¼ cup fresh parsley, chopped (optional)

1. In a large skillet over medium-high heat, heat the oil. Add the beef in a single layer. Season with pepper. Cook for 4 to 5 minutes without disturbing until deeply browned. Flip and brown the opposite side.

2. Sprinkle the flour over the beef. Cook, stirring, for 1 to 2 minutes.

3. Stir in the beef broth, scraping up any browned bits from the bottom of the skillet. Pour the beef and broth into your slow cooker. Add the potatoes, carrots, onion, tomato paste, Italian seasoning, and Worcestershire sauce.

4. Cover the slow cooker and cook on Low heat for 8 hours, or High heat for 4 hours until the beef is tender. Taste and add more pepper, as needed. Garnish with parsley (if using).

5. Refrigerate individual portions in airtight containers for up to 4 days, or freeze for up to 4 months.

* **Prep Ahead:** Cook the beef completely until no pink remains in the center following steps 1 and 2. Transfer to an airtight container. Place the remaining ingredients, except the parsley, in another airtight container and place the parsley in a resealable bag. Refrigerate for up to 5 days.

* **Ingredient Tip:** To save time, I buy pre-cut stew beef. If you prefer, buy a single piece of beef chuck and cut it into 2-inch pieces.

Per Serving: Calories: 288; Protein: 28g; Fat: 11g; Carbohydrates: 19g; Fiber: 4g; Sodium: 178mg

CHAPTER 4

Vegetarian and Vegan

Braised Beans with Tomato and Kale

Serves 8 / Prep Time: 15 minutes / Cook Time: 12 hours (Low)

FREEZER-FRIENDLY GLUTEN-FREE VEGAN

This is the kind of rich stew I crave when it snows. It's warm and satisfying but won't weigh you down. Fennel gives it a hint of sweetness, and garlic and red pepper flakes pack a flavor punch. Serve this dish on its own or dress it up with garlic toast. You can use any white beans in this recipe, but I especially love great northern or cannellini beans.

2 tablespoons olive oil
1 onion, chopped
½ teaspoon kosher salt
1 fennel bulb, thinly sliced
1 teaspoon red
   pepper flakes
10 garlic cloves, chopped
6 cups Vegetable
   Broth (page 134),
   or low-sodium
   vegetable broth
1½ cups dried white beans
1 (15-ounce) can crushed
   tomatoes
1 bunch kale, chopped

1. In a large skillet over medium heat, heat the oil. Add the onion and salt. Cook for 2 to 3 minutes until translucent. Stir in the fennel and cook for 8 minutes until softened. Stir in the red pepper flakes and garlic and cook for 1 minute more. Transfer the vegetables to your slow cooker. Stir in the vegetable broth, beans, and tomatoes.

2. Cover the slow cooker and cook on Low heat for 12 hours, or until the beans are tender.

3. Stir in the kale until softened.

4. Refrigerate individual portions in airtight containers for up to 5 days, or freeze for up to 3 months.

* **Prep Ahead:** Prepare the vegetables as described in step 1, adding them to an airtight container. Stir in the tomatoes. Place the beans and enough water to cover in a second container. Refrigerate for up to 2 days. Drain the beans before cooking. Combine the beans, vegetable mixture, and broth in the slow cooker. Soaking the beans reduces the cooking time to about 8 hours. Add the kale as directed.

* **Substitution Tip:** Swap spinach or chard for the kale, if you prefer a more delicate flavor.

Per Serving: Calories: 215; Protein: 15g; Fat: 8g; Carbohydrates: 35g; Fiber: 12g; Sodium: 655mg

Greek Stuffed Peppers

Serves 6 / Prep Time: 10 minutes / Cook Time: 8 hours (Low); 4 hours (High)

FREEZER-FRIENDLY GLUTEN-FREE VEGETARIAN

Stuffed peppers are one of my favorite things to make because there are just so many different ways to fill them. When you make them in a slow cooker, the peppers become very soft and sweet, almost like roasted red peppers. For this recipe, I play off the roasted red pepper theme and incorporate some of my favorite Greek-inspired ingredients.

1 cup quinoa, rinsed

½ cup Vegetable Broth (page 134), or low-sodium vegetable broth

2 cups fresh baby spinach, chopped

½ cup pitted Kalamata olives, whole

4 ounces feta cheese, crumbled

1 (14-ounce) can chickpeas, drained and rinsed

1 shallot, minced

2 teaspoons dried oregano

6 red, orange, or yellow bell peppers, tops removed, seeded

1. In a medium bowl, stir together the quinoa, vegetable broth, spinach, olives, cheese, chickpeas, shallot, and oregano. Let sit for 5 minutes. Scoop the mixture into the hollowed-out peppers. Stand the peppers upright in your slow cooker.

2. Cover the slow cooker and cook on Low heat for 8 hours, or High heat for 4 hours.

3. Using a spatula, carefully transfer each pepper to an individual airtight container. Refrigerate for up to 5 days, or freeze for up to 3 months. For best results, reheat in a 350°F oven for 20 to 30 minutes.

Prep Ahead: Complete step 1. Arrange the peppers in a wide, shallow container—I find a baking dish works well. Cover and refrigerate for up to 3 days.

Ingredient Tip: Red and orange bell peppers are sweeter than green bell peppers, which have a sharp, slightly bitter taste. For this recipe, look for peppers with wide, flat bottoms so they stand well on their own. If needed, trim a thin slice from the bottom to help them stand.

Per Serving: Calories: 304; Protein: 12g; Fat: 9g; Carbohydrates: 45g; Fiber: 8g; Sodium: 479mg

Tofu Fried Rice

Serves 10 / Prep Time: 10 minutes / Cook Time: 8 hours (Low)

FREEZER-FRIENDLY   VEGAN

Tofu works surprisingly well in the slow cooker. It doesn't fall apart or turn to mush as you might expect but, instead, stays firm with a slightly chewy texture. It doesn't have much flavor on its own, so I added plenty of garlic, ginger, and chili paste to season this "fried" rice.

1 tablespoon olive oil

1 pound extra-firm tofu, diced

3 garlic cloves, minced

1 tablespoon grated peeled fresh ginger

4 cups Vegetable Broth (page 134), or low-sodium vegetable broth

2 cups long-grain brown rice

1 pound mixed vegetables

¼ cup low-sodium soy sauce

3 tablespoons sesame oil

2 tablespoons chili paste

1. In a skillet over high heat, heat the olive oil. Add the tofu and cook for 2 to 3 minutes per side until browned. Stir in the garlic and ginger. Cook for 1 minute. Transfer the tofu to your slow cooker. Stir in the vegetable broth, brown rice, vegetables, soy sauce, sesame oil, and chili paste.

2. Cover the slow cooker and cook on Low heat for 8 hours.

3. Refrigerate individual portions in airtight containers for up to 5 days, or freeze for up to 3 months.

✷ **Prep Ahead:** Cook the tofu as instructed in step 1. Place it in an airtight container, along with the rice, vegetables, soy sauce, sesame oil, and chili paste. Store the broth in a separate container. Refrigerate for up to 5 days.

✷ **Ingredient Tip:** To keep things simple, I buy pre-mixed vegetables for this recipe. A mixture of peas, carrots, green beans, and corn is great, but you can use whatever combination you like.

Per Serving: Calories: 250; Protein: 10g; Fat: 9g; Carbohydrates: 35g; Fiber: 3g; Sodium: 306mg

Buffalo Chickpea Sloppy Joes

Serves 6 / **Prep Time: 5 minutes** / **Cook Time: 8 hours (Low); 3 hours (High)**

VEGAN

These sloppy Joes have all the flavor of Buffalo wings, right down to the carrots and celery, but they also include a crispy slaw to add a little crunch. Frank's RedHot brand sauce gives this recipe the most authentic flavor. Be sure to get the original RedHot sauce, which is made with just cayenne peppers, vinegar, salt, and garlic powder.

5 cups Vegetable
  Broth (page 134),
  or low-sodium
  vegetable broth
1½ cups dried chickpeas
3 carrots, finely diced
3 celery stalks, chopped
½ cup hot sauce (such as
  Frank's RedHot)
2 tablespoons
  tomato paste
1 cup coleslaw mix
Juice of 1 lime
2 tablespoons chopped
  fresh cilantro
¼ teaspoon kosher salt
6 vegan hamburger rolls,
  preferably whole wheat

1. In your slow cooker, stir together the vegetable broth, chickpeas, carrots, celery, hot sauce, and tomato paste.

2. Cover the slow cooker and cook on Low heat for 8 hours, or High heat for 3 hours.

3. In a small bowl, stir together the coleslaw mix, lime juice, cilantro, and salt.

4. Refrigerate individual portions of the chickpeas and slaw, each in separate airtight containers, for up to 4 days. Serve the chickpeas on the hamburger rolls, topped with the slaw.

✢ **Prep Ahead:** You'll need 3 airtight containers to prep this recipe: 1 for the sauce, 1 for the chickpeas, and 1 for the slaw. Combine the broth, carrots, celery, hot sauce, and tomato paste in the first container. In the second, combine the chickpeas with enough water to cover. Finally, combine the coleslaw mix, lime juice, cilantro, and salt in the third container. Refrigerate for up to 2 days.

Per Serving: Calories: 288; Protein: 15g; Fat: 4g; Carbohydrates: 54g; Fiber: 11g; Sodium: 1,194mg

Italian Spaghetti Squash

Serves 6 / Prep Time: 10 minutes / Cook Time: 8 hours (Low)

FREEZER-FRIENDLY GLUTEN-FREE ONE-POT VEGETARIAN

Spaghetti squash is so good, but it can take a really long time to cook in the oven. Why not let the slow cooker take care of it while you go about your day? In this recipe, the squash cooks right in a thick tomato sauce. I love adding mushrooms and spinach at the end for extra nutrition. If you prefer, use jarred tomato-basil sauce instead of making your own; my go-to favorite brands include Rao's and Classico.

3 cups Marinara Sauce (page 135), or jarred tomato-basil sauce

1 (28-ounce) can diced tomatoes with juice

1 tablespoon Italian seasoning

¼ cup whole Kalamata olives, pitted (optional)

2 tablespoons capers, drained (optional)

1 large spaghetti squash, halved crosswise (see tip), seeds and pulp removed

1 pint cremini mushrooms, sliced

3 ounces fresh baby spinach

3 ounces shredded mozzarella cheese

1. In your slow cooker, combine the marinara, tomatoes with their juices, and Italian seasoning. Stir in the olives (if using) and capers (if using).

2. Nestle the squash, cut-side down, into the sauce.

3. Cover the slow cooker and cook on Low heat for 8 hours.

4. Carefully remove the squash from the slow cooker (it will be very soft). Using a fork, scrape the inner fibers into a colander over the sink; discard the shell.

5. Stir the mushrooms and spinach into the sauce, then add the squash strands. Top with the mozzarella.

6. If the sauce is too thin, cook on Low heat, uncovered, for 20 to 30 minutes more.

7. Refrigerate individual portions in airtight containers for up to 5 days, or freeze for up to 3 months.

* **Prep Ahead:** You'll need two medium airtight containers for this recipe. Combine the marinara, tomatoes, olives (if using), and capers (if using) in one container. In the second, place the mozzarella on the bottom, and top with the mushrooms and spinach. Refrigerate for up to 5 days. Prepare the squash immediately before cooking.
* **Cooking Tip:** I find it's easiest to fit the squash into a slow cooker if you halve it crosswise into rounds (not lengthwise into boats).

Per Serving: Calories: 145; Protein: 10g; Fat: 3g; Carbohydrates: 21g; Fiber: 5g; Sodium: 624mg

Thai Curry Noodles

Serves 6 / Prep Time: 5 minutes / Cook Time: 8 hours, 30 minutes (Low) plus 2 hours, 30 minutes (High)

FREEZER-FRIENDLY   ONE-POT   VEGAN

Rice noodles are perfect for making in the slow cooker because they only need to be soaked in hot water (or other hot liquid) for a few minutes to soften. You don't have to take time to boil them in a separate pot. In this recipe, a spicy Thai vegetable curry simmers all day so that the flavors have time to come together. Dried noodles are added just before serving.

2 cups water

1 (14-ounce) can full-fat coconut milk

5 tablespoons curry paste

1 tablespoon grated peeled fresh ginger

2 teaspoons low-sodium soy sauce

1 onion, sliced

2 bell peppers, any color, seeded and sliced

5 cups broccoli florets

8 ounces pad Thai rice noodles

¼ cup fresh basil leaves, chopped

Juice of 2 limes

1. In your slow cooker, stir together the water, coconut milk, curry paste, ginger, and soy sauce. Add the onion, bell peppers, and broccoli.

2. Cover the slow cooker and cook on Low heat for 8 hours, or High heat for 2 hours.

3. Add the noodles to the slow cooker, being sure to submerge them in the sauce. Re-cover the cooker and cook on Low heat for 20 to 30 minutes more until the noodles soften. Stir in the basil and lime juice.

4. Refrigerate individual portions in airtight containers for up to 5 days, or freeze for up to 3 months.

* **Prep Ahead:** Combine the water, coconut milk, curry, ginger, and soy sauce in an airtight container. Add the onion, bell peppers, and broccoli to a second airtight container. Refrigerate for up to 5 days, or freeze for up to 3 months. If frozen, thaw the ingredients overnight in the refrigerator before adding to your slow cooker.

* **Substitution Tip:** If you prefer, serve this curry over Brown Rice (page 145) instead of noodles.

Per Serving: Calories: 321; Protein: 5g; Fat: 12g; Carbohydrates: 44g; Fiber: 4g; Sodium: 574mg

Sweet Potato Stew

Serves 6 / **Prep Time: 10 minutes** / **Cook Time: 8 hours (Low)**

FREEZER-FRIENDLY GLUTEN-FREE ONE-POT VEGAN

I love sweet and spicy flavors, and this recipe is just that, using inspirational New World flavors. The poblano pepper adds heat as a balance to the sweetness of the sweet potatoes, and cumin adds an earthy note. This stew is great on its own, but you can make it extra special by topping it with a dollop of sour cream or plain Greek yogurt.

6 sweet potatoes, peeled and cubed

4 cups Vegetable Broth (page 134), or low-sodium vegetable broth

1 (14.5-ounce) can fire-roasted diced tomatoes, drained

1 red onion, diced

4 garlic cloves, minced

1 poblano pepper, diced

1 teaspoon ground cumin

½ teaspoon kosher salt

½ teaspoon freshly ground black pepper

4 cups fresh baby spinach

1. In your slow cooker, combine the sweet potatoes, vegetable broth, tomatoes, red onion, garlic, poblano, cumin, salt, and pepper.

2. Cover the slow cooker and cook on Low heat for 8 hours.

3. Stir in the spinach until wilted.

4. Refrigerate individual portions in airtight containers for up to 5 days, or freeze for up to 3 months.

✤ **Prep Ahead:** In an airtight container, combine the ingredients as instructed in step 1, making sure the sweet potatoes are completely submerged in the liquid. Refrigerate for up to 4 days. Do not freeze before cooking, as the texture of the sweet potatoes will change.

Per Serving: Calories: 179; Protein: 5g; Fat: 1g; Carbohydrates: 40g; Fiber: 6g; Sodium: 374mg

Tex-Mex Quinoa

Serves 6 / Prep Time: 5 minutes / Cook Time: 8 hours (Low)

FREEZER-FRIENDLY GLUTEN-FREE ONE-POT VEGETARIAN

This Tex-Mex casserole is chock-full of flavor, thanks to the addition of salsa, chili powder, and corn. Quinoa and beans are both good sources of protein, so this hearty casserole will keep you full for a while. I love packing this one for lunches to help fuel my afternoons. I always get compliments on how good it smells when I heat it up!

1 cup quinoa, rinsed

2 cups Vegetable Broth (page 134), or low-sodium vegetable broth

1 cup fresh salsa

1 (15.5-ounce) can low-sodium black beans, drained and rinsed

1 cup corn

1 teaspoon chili powder

1 cup shredded Cheddar cheese

¼ cup fresh cilantro, chopped

1 lime, cut into 6 wedges

1. In your slow cooker, combine the quinoa, vegetable broth, salsa, black beans, corn, and chili powder.

2. Cover the slow cooker and cook on Low heat for 8 hours.

3. Top with the cheese and cilantro.

4. Place individual portions in airtight containers and squeeze 1 lime wedge over each portion. Refrigerate for up to 5 days, or freeze for up to 3 months.

- **Prep Ahead:** Measure the quinoa into an airtight container. In a second container, combine the broth, salsa, beans, corn, and chili powder. Measure the cheese and cilantro into a third. Refrigerate for up to 5 days, or freeze for up to 3 months. If you plan to make the quinoa within the week, store the lime, whole, at room temperature and cut just before serving. If you plan to freeze this recipe for later, cut the lime into wedges and freeze in the same container as the cheese and cilantro (remove the lime wedges before adding the cheese to the slow cooker). If frozen, thaw the ingredients in the refrigerator overnight before adding to your slow cooker.
- **Ingredient Tip:** Quinoa naturally has a very bitter coating, which keeps predators like birds away. These days, most quinoa is sold pre-rinsed, but it never hurts to give it a good rinse to be sure. Add the quinoa to a strainer and run cool water over it until the water runs clear.

Per Serving: Calories: 293; Protein: 14g; Fat: 9g; Carbohydrates: 41g; Fiber: 8g; Sodium: 394mg

Pad Thai Spaghetti Squash

Serves 6 / Prep Time: 10 minutes / Cook Time: 8 hours (Low)

VEGAN

Traditionally, pad Thai gets its unique sweet-tart flavor from tamarind paste. Unfortunately, it can be tricky to find, and you often end up with way more than you need. Sugar-free ketchup works nicely as a substitute. To give this recipe body, I melt peanut butter into the sauce. I prefer using natural peanut butter without added sugar.

¼ cup peanut butter

¼ cup sugar-free ketchup

Juice of 2 limes

2 garlic cloves, minced

1 teaspoon minced peeled fresh ginger

3 tablespoons low-sodium soy sauce

4 carrots, diced

2 red bell peppers, seeded and sliced

1 red onion, thinly sliced

1 spaghetti squash, halved crosswise, seeds and pulp removed

¼ cup chopped peanuts

1. In a small bowl, whisk the peanut butter, ketchup, lime juice, garlic, ginger, and soy sauce into a smooth sauce.

2. In your slow cooker, combine the carrots, red bell peppers, and red onion. Pour the sauce over the vegetables. Place the squash on top, cut-side down.

3. Cover the slow cooker and cook on Low heat for 8 hours.

4. Carefully remove the squash from the slow cooker. Stir the sauce to smooth out any lumps. Using a fork, scrape the inner fibers of the squash into a colander over the sink; discard the shell.

5. Return the squash strands to the slow cooker and stir to combine. Sprinkle the peanuts over the top.

6. Refrigerate individual portions in airtight containers for up to 5 days. Do not freeze because the squash will become mushy.

✳ **Prep Ahead:** Prepare the sauce as directed in step 1 and transfer to an airtight container, along with the carrots, red bell peppers, and red onion. Refrigerate for up to 3 days. Prepare the squash immediately before cooking.

Per Serving: Calories: 181; Protein: 7g; Fat: 9g; Carbohydrates: 20g; Fiber: 5g; Sodium: 462mg

Chickpea Curry

Serves 6 / **Prep Time: 10 minutes** / **Cook Time: 8 hours (Low); 3 hours (High)**

FREEZER-FRIENDLY   GLUTEN-FREE   VEGAN

Indian curries are perfect for meal prep as their saucy base freezes and reheats really well. They also benefit from the long cooking times with a slow cooker, which gives the flavors plenty of time to come together. I eat this curry on its own like a stew, but you can also serve it with cauliflower rice or flatbread.

1 tablespoon olive oil

1 onion, sliced

4 garlic cloves, minced

1 tablespoon grated peeled fresh ginger

1½ tablespoons garam masala

½ teaspoon ground turmeric

¼ cup tomato paste

1 (29-ounce) can chickpeas, drained and rinsed

1 (14.5-ounce) can diced tomatoes, drained

1½ cups full-fat coconut milk

1. In a large skillet over medium heat, heat the oil. Add the onion and cook for 3 to 4 minutes until translucent. Stir in the garlic, ginger, garam masala, and turmeric. Cook for 1 minute. Stir in the tomato paste and cook for 1 minute more. Scrape the onion and spice mixture into your slow cooker. Stir in the chickpeas, tomatoes, and coconut milk.

2. Cover the slow cooker and cook on Low heat for 8 hours, or High heat for 3 hours.

3. Refrigerate individual portions in airtight containers for up to 5 days, or freeze for up to 3 months.

Prep Ahead: Sauté the onion and spices as instructed in step 1. Scrape into an airtight container. Add the chickpeas, tomatoes, and coconut milk. Refrigerate up to 5 days, or freeze up to 3 months. If frozen, thaw the ingredients overnight in the refrigerator before adding to your slow cooker.

Cooking Tip: If you're in a rush, skip sautéing the onion and spices in step 1 and add them right to the slow cooker, but you'll sacrifice some flavor.

Per Serving: Calories: 306; Protein: 9g; Fat: 14g; Carbohydrates: 35g; Fiber: 9g; Sodium: 395mg

Zucchini Lasagna

Serves 6 / Prep Time: 15 minutes / Cook Time: 8 hours (Low); 3 hours (High)

GLUTEN-FREE   VEGETARIAN

Thin strips of zucchini stand in for noodles in this take on lasagna. Zucchini releases a lot of moisture as it cooks, so be sure not to skip step 1. Cooking the zucchini for a few minutes on the stovetop will help dry out the zucchini as excess water evaporates. Bell peppers and fresh basil add extra flavor to the sauce.

1 tablespoon olive oil

4 zucchini, cut into ¼-inch-thick slices

1 pound reduced-fat ricotta

2 large eggs

2 cups Marinara Sauce (page 135), or jarred pasta sauce of choice

1 red or orange bell pepper, seeded and diced

2 tablespoons chopped fresh basil leaves

2 cups shredded mozzarella cheese

1. In a large skillet over medium heat, heat the oil. Add the zucchini slices in a single layer (working in batches if needed) and cook for 2 to 3 minutes per side until lightly browned and dry.

2. In a medium bowl, whisk the ricotta and eggs to blend. In a second bowl, stir together the marinara, red bell peppers, and basil.

3. Start building the lasagna: Lightly coat the bottom of your slow cooker with a few tablespoons of marinara. Add a single layer of zucchini slices. Top the zucchini with one-third of the remaining marinara. Layer half the ricotta mixture over the sauce. Repeat with another layer of zucchini, marinara, and ricotta. Sprinkle the mozzarella over the top.

4. Wrap the slow cooker lid with a clean kitchen towel to trap condensation and cover the slow cooker with it. Cook on Low heat for 8 hours, or High heat for 3 hours.

5. Remove the lid and let stand for 15 minutes before serving. This will allow any liquid released during the cooking process to be reabsorbed.

6. Refrigerate individual portions in airtight containers for up to 5 days.

CONTINUED ››

Zucchini Lasagna CONTINUED

❋ **Prep Ahead:** Prepare the lasagna in a large airtight container with a slow cooker liner through step 3, rather than in your slow cooker. Refrigerate for up to 4 days. When you're ready to cook the lasagna, carefully lift the liner out of the container and transfer it to your slow cooker. Do not freeze because raw zucchini doesn't freeze well.

❋ **Ingredient Tip:** Marinara Sauce (page 135) is wonderful in this recipe, but you can use any good quality pasta sauce as long as there are no added sugars or other flavors.

Per Serving: Calories: 301; Protein: 24g; Fat: 17g; Carbohydrates: 16g; Fiber: 3g; Sodium: 544mg

Chipotle Barbecue Jackfruit Tacos

Serves 6 / Prep Time: 5 minutes / Cook Time: 8 hours (Low); 4 hours (High)

FREEZER-FRIENDLY   GLUTEN-FREE   VEGAN

Jackfruit is kind of amazing. It's a tropical fruit related to figs and breadfruit, but the unripe fruit has a very mild flavor and a stringy texture that's the perfect stand-in for shredded chicken or pork. You won't believe how meat-like it is. The fresh fruit is very sticky and difficult to work with, but canned young jackfruit packed in water or brine is becoming easier to find in grocery stores.

3 (20-ounce) cans young
  jackfruit in water,
  drained and rinsed
2 cups tomato sauce
½ cup pure maple syrup
1 canned chipotle in
  adobo sauce, minced
Juice of 1 orange
Juice of 2 limes, divided
1 cup coleslaw mix
4 radishes, thinly sliced
1 tablespoon olive oil
18 small corn tortillas

1. In your slow cooker, combine the jackfruit, tomato sauce, maple syrup, chipotle, orange juice, and the juice of 1 lime.

2. Cover the slow cooker and cook on Low heat for 8 hours, or High heat for 4 hours. Using a spoon, gently mash the jackfruit, coaxing it into shreds.

3. In a medium bowl, stir together the coleslaw mix, radishes, oil, and remaining juice of 1 lime.

4. Portion the jackfruit into individual airtight containers and the slaw into separate individual containers. Refrigerate for up to 5 days. Serve the jackfruit and slaw in the tortillas.

   ✦ **Prep Ahead:** In an airtight container, combine the tomato sauce, maple syrup, chipotle, orange juice, and the juice of 1 lime. In a second container, combine the slaw mix, radishes, oil, and remaining lime juice. Store the jackfruit separately. Refrigerate for up to 5 days.

   ✦ **Cooking Tip:** The barbecue jackfruit can be frozen for up to 3 months. The slaw does not freeze well and is best prepared the week you plan to eat this.

Per Serving: Calories: 277; Protein: 4g; Fat: 6g; Carbohydrates: 57g; Fiber: 10g; Sodium: 959mg

Chickpea Tagine

Serves 6 / **Prep Time: 5 minutes** / **Cook Time: 8 hours (Low); 3 hours (High)**

FREEZER-FRIENDLY GLUTEN-FREE ONE-POT VEGAN

Tagines are traditional clay pots with cone-shaped lids that minimize evaporation and direct condensation back onto the food cooking inside. In this way, they're very similar to modern slow cookers. North African cuisine is famous for its generous use of spices and dried fruit. If you've never tried it, some of the flavors might sound intimidating, but I promise it all works together really well.

1 (29-ounce) can chickpeas, drained and rinsed
1 (14.5-ounce) can diced tomatoes, drained
1 (14-ounce) can artichokes, drained
1 tablespoon ras el hanout
2 cups fresh baby spinach
¼ cup pitted green olives, whole
2 tablespoons raisins

1. In your slow cooker, combine the chickpeas, tomatoes, artichokes, and ras el hanout.

2. Cover the slow cooker and cook on Low heat for 8 hours, or High heat for 3 hours.

3. Stir in the spinach, olives, and raisins. Let sit for 5 to 10 minutes, or until the spinach is wilted.

4. Refrigerate individual portions in airtight containers for up to 5 days, or freeze for up to 3 months.

* **Prep Ahead:** In an airtight container, combine the chickpeas, tomatoes, artichokes, and seasoning. In a second container, mix the spinach, olives, and raisins. Refrigerate for up to 5 days, or freeze for up to 6 months. If frozen, thaw the ingredients in the refrigerator overnight before adding to your slow cooker.

* **Ingredient Tip:** Ras el hanout is a flavorful Arabic spice blend made with warm spices. The individual ingredients can vary but typically include cardamom, cumin, cinnamon, allspice, ginger, and turmeric. Premixed blends can be found easily online or in most major grocery stores.

Per Serving: Calories: 205; Protein: 9g; Fat: 3g; Carbohydrates: 36g; Fiber: 10g; Sodium: 559mg

Butternut Squash Macaroni and Cheese

Serves 8 / **Prep Time: 10 minutes** / **Cook Time: 8½ hours (Low); 2½ hours plus 30 minutes (High)**

FREEZER-FRIENDLY   ONE-POT   VEGETARIAN

Butternut squash cooks down into a thick sauce, so you don't need to use as much cheese. I like Asiago cheese because its sharp flavor stands up to the sweetness of the squash. Serve this macaroni and cheese with lots of freshly ground black pepper.

1 butternut squash, peeled and diced

1½ cups Chicken Stock (page 132), or low-sodium chicken broth

1 small onion, chopped

3 garlic cloves, minced

½ cup milk

4 ounces Asiago cheese, shredded

1 pound whole-grain elbow macaroni

1. In your slow cooker, combine the squash, chicken stock, onion, and garlic.

2. Cover the slow cooker and cook on Low heat for 8½ hours, or High heat for 2½ hours.

3. Using an immersion blender or potato masher, blend the squash into a smooth sauce.

4. Stir in the milk and cheese.

5. Add the macaroni. Re-cover the cooker and cook on High heat for 30 minutes until cooked through.

6. Refrigerate individual portions in airtight containers for up to 5 days, or freeze for up to 3 months.

* **Prep Ahead:** Prepare the ingredients as instructed in step 1, adding them to an airtight container. Measure the milk and cheese into a second container. Refrigerate for up to 5 days.

* **Substitution Tip:** For an additional nutrition boost, stir in some peas or fresh baby spinach before step 6.

Per Serving: Calories: 314; Protein: 15g; Fat: 6g; Carbohydrates: 51g; Fiber: 8g; Sodium: 273mg

Root Vegetable Potpie

Serves 6 / Prep Time: 15 minutes / Cook Time: 8 hours (Low); 4 hours plus 30 minutes (High)

DAIRY-FREE　FREEZER-FRIENDLY　VEGETARIAN

Potpie is probably one of the more surprising recipes that can be made in a slow cooker. I use pre-made piecrust to keep things simple. Wholly Wholesome makes a really good organic, dairy-free crust made with whole-wheat flour. If you use a different brand, double-check the ingredients to make sure it's vegetarian, if that's important to you.

3 potatoes, diced

3 carrots, cut into coins

3 celery stalks,
   thinly sliced

1 parsnip, cut into coins

1 cup peas

2 teaspoons dried thyme

½ teaspoon freshly
   ground black pepper

2 cups Vegetable
   Broth (page 134),
   or low-sodium
   vegetable broth

¼ cup cornstarch

¼ cup water

1 refrigerated piecrust,
   preferably whole grain

1. In your slow cooker, combine the potatoes, carrots, celery, parsnip, peas, thyme, pepper, and vegetable broth.

2. Cover the slow cooker and cook on Low heat for 8 hours, or High heat for 4 hours.

3. In a small bowl, whisk the cornstarch and water to make a slurry. Stir the slurry into the vegetables.

4. Place the piecrust over the vegetables and poke a few holes in the crust to let the steam escape.

5. Wrap the slow cooker lid with a clean kitchen towel to trap condensation and cover the slow cooker with it. Cook on High heat for 30 to 40 minutes until the crust is cooked through.

6. Refrigerate individual portions in airtight containers for up to 5 days, or freeze for up to 2 months. For best results, reheat in the oven to crisp the crust.

- **Prep Ahead:** In an airtight container, combine the ingredients as in step 1. Keep the pie-crust separate from the remaining ingredients until ready to cook the pie. Refrigerate for up to 5 days, or freeze for up to 3 months. If frozen, thaw the ingredients overnight in the refrigerator before adding to your slow cooker.
- **Substitution Tip:** Swap the parsnip for either a diced turnip or 1 cup of trimmed fresh green beans.

Per Serving: Calories: 261; Protein: 5g; Fat: 7g; Carbohydrates: 45g; Fiber: 6g; Sodium: 226mg

Mushroom and Barley "Risotto"

Serves 6 / **Prep Time: 10 minutes** / **Cook Time: 6 hours (Low)**

FREEZER-FRIENDLY   VEGETARIAN

Many people only use barley in soups, but this grain is delicious as the base for salads or hearty dishes, like this "risotto." Barley has a tender, chewy texture and releases starches into the liquid as it cooks, giving the finished dish a creamy, risotto-like feel. Cremini mushrooms are easy to find, but you can use a mixture of your favorites, if you prefer. I love using a combination of porcini, chanterelle, and oyster mushrooms when they're in season.

1 tablespoon olive oil

1 onion, diced

4 garlic cloves, minced

2 pints cremini mushrooms, sliced

2 tablespoons finely chopped fresh sage leaves

½ teaspoon kosher salt

½ teaspoon freshly ground black pepper, plus more for seasoning

1¼ cups dried barley

3 cups Vegetable Broth (page 134), or low-sodium vegetable broth

¼ cup grated Parmesan cheese

2 cups frozen peas

2 tablespoons heavy (whipping) cream (optional)

1. In a sauté pan or skillet over medium heat, heat the oil. Add the onion and cook for 3 to 4 minutes until softened. Stir in the garlic and cook for 1 minute.

2. Add the mushrooms and cook for 5 minutes, stirring frequently, until deeply browned and softened. Stir in the sage. Season with salt and pepper.

3. In your slow cooker, combine the barley and vegetable broth. Stir in the mushroom mixture.

4. Cover the slow cooker and cook on Low heat for 6 hours until the barley is tender.

5. Stir in the Parmesan, peas, and heavy cream (if using). Let sit for 5 minutes until the peas are warm. Taste and season with more pepper, as needed.

6. Refrigerate individual portions in airtight containers for up to 5 days, or freeze for up to 3 months.

* **Prep Ahead:** Cook the mushrooms, garlic, and onion as directed in steps 1 and 2. Transfer to an airtight container. Pour in the vegetable broth. Measure the barley into a second container and the Parmesan, peas, and cream (if using) into a third. Refrigerate for up to 3 days, or freeze for up to 6 months without the heavy cream. If frozen, thaw the ingredients in the refrigerator overnight before adding to your slow cooker.
* **Ingredient Tip:** Mushrooms give off a lot of liquid as they cook, so be sure to sauté them before adding to the slow cooker. This will help reduce some of that liquid so that you won't end up with watery risotto.

Per Serving: Calories: 257; Protein: 11g; Fat: 5g; Carbohydrates: 44g; Fiber: 10g; Sodium: 603mg

CHAPTER 5

Seafood and Poultry

Shrimp Fajitas

Serves 6 / Prep Time: 10 minutes / Cook Time: 8 hours (Low); 2 hours (High)

DAIRY-FREE   FREEZER-FRIENDLY

Fajitas are one of my favorite dinners. They're usually a quick stir-fry, but for this recipe, I've gone in the opposite direction. Cooking the vegetables low and slow gives the onion time to caramelize and the peppers time to infuse the simple tomato sauce with tons of flavor. I top these shrimp fajitas with a simple take on guacamole, but you can swap in your favorite toppings.

Nonstick cooking spray

3 bell peppers, any color, seeded and sliced

1 red onion, sliced

2 garlic cloves, minced

1 (10-ounce) can diced tomatoes with green chilies, drained

1 tablespoon low-sodium soy sauce

2 pounds raw shrimp, peeled

2 avocados, halved and pitted

Juice of 1 lime

¼ cup fresh cilantro, chopped

12 small corn tortillas

1. Coat your slow cooker with cooking spray and add the bell peppers, red onion, garlic, tomatoes and green chilies, and soy sauce.

2. Cover the slow cooker and cook on Low heat for 8 hours, or High heat for 2 hours.

3. Add the shrimp to the slow cooker. Re-cover the cooker and cook on High heat for 10 to 15 minutes until the shrimp are pink, opaque, and cooked through.

4. Scoop the avocado flesh into a small bowl. Add the lime juice and cilantro. Mash to combine.

5. Refrigerate individual portions of the fajita filling in airtight containers. Store the mashed avocado in a separate container, smoothing out the top as much as possible and topping with a thin layer of water to prevent oxidation (pour the water off before serving). Refrigerate for up to 4 days, or freeze for up to 6 months. Serve the shrimp mixture in the tortillas, topped with the mashed avocado.

* **Prep Ahead:** In an airtight container, combine the bell peppers, onion, garlic, tomatoes, and soy sauce. In a separate container, mash together the avocados, lime juice, and cilantro; smooth the top as much as you can and top with a thin layer of water. Keep the shrimp packed separately until ready to cook. Refrigerate for up to 2 days.
* **Ingredient Tip:** If using frozen shrimp, run them under cool water for 10 minutes to thaw before adding to the slow cooker. Soy sauce isn't a traditional ingredient in fajitas, but it adds a deep, savory note to the filling that can otherwise be lacking.

Per Serving: Calories: 355; Protein: 35g; Fat: 14g; Carbohydrates: 26g; Fiber: 6g; Sodium: 640mg

Red Curry Shrimp

Serves 6 / Prep Time: 10 minutes / Cook Time: 8 hours (Low); 2 hours (High)

DAIRY-FREE FREEZER-FRIENDLY GLUTEN-FREE ONE-POT

The red curry ramen that I created for my first cookbook is one of my favorite recipes of all time. Shiitake mushrooms, sesame oil, and rice vinegar add a ton of depth to the rich broth. Here, I've added those ingredients to a more traditional red curry shrimp recipe. The broth and vegetables cook low and slow all day, but the shrimp and rice are added just before serving so that they don't overcook.

1 (14-ounce) can
   coconut milk
3½ ounces shiitake
   mushrooms, sliced
2 tablespoons red
   curry paste
2 tablespoons sesame oil
1 tablespoon rice vinegar
1 tablespoon grated
   lime zest
2 red bell peppers, seeded
   and sliced
2 cups fresh
   broccoli florets
2 pounds raw
   shrimp, peeled
1 cup instant brown rice
¼ cup fresh basil
   leaves, chopped

1. In your slow cooker, whisk the coconut milk, mushrooms, red curry paste, oil, vinegar, and lime zest until smooth. Add the red bell peppers and broccoli.

2. Cover the slow cooker and cook on Low heat for 8 hours, or High heat for 2 hours.

3. Gently stir in the shrimp, brown rice, and basil. Re-cover the cooker and cook for 10 to 15 minutes more, or until the shrimp are pink, opaque, and cooked through and the rice is tender.

4. Refrigerate individual portions in airtight containers for up to 4 days, or freeze for up to 4 months.

   ✴ **Prep Ahead:** Combine the coconut milk, mushrooms, curry paste, oil, rice vinegar, lime zest, bell peppers, and broccoli in an airtight container. Refrigerate for up to 5 days, or freeze for up to 3 months. Keep the shrimp, rice, and basil separate until ready to cook. If frozen, thaw the ingredients in the refrigerator overnight before adding to your slow cooker.

   ✴ **Substitution Tip:** If you prefer, swap the shrimp for boneless, skinless chicken breasts. Add the chicken along with the vegetables in step 1 and reduce the cooking time to 6 hours on Low.

Per Serving: Calories: 402; Protein: 34g; Fat: 19g; Carbohydrates: 21g; Fiber: 3g; Sodium: 339mg

Pesto Salmon with Farro

Serves 6 / Prep Time: 5 minutes / Cook Time: 6 hours plus 1½ hours (Low)

5-INGREDIENT   DAIRY-FREE   FREEZER-FRIENDLY   ONE-POT

Salmon in the slow cooker? I know it sounds crazy, but it actually works—it's similar to steaming the fish. Plus, the moist heat keeps the salmon tender and flaky. Cooking fish all day isn't a great idea because it will overcook and it smells bad. Luckily, salmon cooks quickly, so you can slip a few fillets into the pot when you get home. Leftovers are great reheated or served chilled on a salad.

1½ cups farro

4 cups Chicken Stock (page 132), or low-sodium chicken broth

½ cup pesto

6 salmon fillets

¼ teaspoon kosher salt

¼ teaspoon freshly ground black pepper

1½ cups cherry tomatoes, halved

1. In your slow cooker, combine the farro, chicken stock, and pesto.

2. Cover the slow cooker and cook on Low heat for 6 hours.

3. Place the salmon fillets on top of the farro. Season with salt and pepper. Re-cover the cooker and cook on Low heat for 1 to 1½ hours, or until the salmon is cooked to your liking.

4. Stir in the tomatoes.

5. Refrigerate individual portions in airtight containers for up to 4 days, or freeze for up to 4 months.

   * **Prep Ahead:** This recipe is simple to prepare, but measuring your ingredients in advance can save time if your mornings are rushed. Measure the farro into an airtight container. Mix the broth and pesto together in a second container. Refrigerate for up to 5 days. The salmon will keep refrigerated for up to 2 days, or frozen for up to 3 months. If frozen, thaw the ingredients in the refrigerator overnight before adding to your slow cooker.

   * **Ingredient Tip:** To save time, cook the salmon ahead (see Poached Salmon, page 141). Reduce the cooking time in step 3 to 10 minutes, or until the salmon is warm.

Per Serving: Calories: 411; Protein: 33g; Fat: 14g; Carbohydrates: 38g; Fiber: 5g; Sodium: 427mg

Chicken with Peppers and Olives

Serves 6 / Prep Time: 5 minutes / Cook Time: 8 hours (Low); 3 hours (High)

DAIRY-FREE FREEZER-FRIENDLY GLUTEN-FREE ONE-POT

This combination of chicken stewed with peppers, tomatoes, and onions is a riff on chicken cacciatore. Fire-roasted crushed tomatoes add depth to the otherwise simple sauce, and the olives and parsley stirred in at the end add a pop of bright, fresh flavor. Serve this stew on its own or over Mashed Potatoes (page 143).

1 (28-ounce) can fire-roasted crushed tomatoes

2 green bell peppers, seeded and sliced

1 pint cremini mushrooms, quartered

3 garlic cloves, minced

1 onion, sliced

6 boneless, skinless chicken thighs

½ teaspoon kosher salt

½ teaspoon freshly ground black pepper

½ cup pitted green olives, chopped

¼ cup fresh parsley, chopped

1. In your slow cooker, combine the tomatoes, green bell peppers, mushrooms, garlic, and onion. Season the chicken with salt and pepper, then add it to the tomato mixture.

2. Cover the slow cooker and cook on Low heat for 8 hours, or High heat for 3 hours.

3. Stir in the olives and parsley.

4. Refrigerate individual portions in airtight containers for up to 4 days, or freeze for up to 4 months.

* **Prep Ahead:** Season the chicken thighs with salt and pepper and place them in an airtight container. Add the tomatoes, bell peppers, mushrooms, onion, and garlic. Measure the olives and parsley into a second container. Refrigerate for up to 2 days, or freeze for up to 3 months. If frozen, thaw the ingredients in the refrigerator overnight before adding to your slow cooker.

* **Substitution Tip:** If you prefer boneless, skinless chicken breasts, reduce the cooking time to 6 hours on Low.

Per Serving: Calories: 208; Protein: 22g; Fat: 10g; Carbohydrates: 12g; Fiber: 3g; Sodium: 703mg

Lemon Chicken

Serves 6 / Prep Time: 5 minutes / Cook Time: 6 hours (Low); 2 hours (High)

DAIRY-FREE FREEZER-FRIENDLY GLUTEN-FREE ONE-POT

This lemon chicken recipe is loosely based on chicken piccata, a classic Italian dish with sautéed chicken in a rich lemon sauce. I love the pop of salty flavor the capers add, but you can replace them with olives or leave them out entirely. If you omit the capers, season the sauce with kosher or sea salt before serving.

Juice of 2 lemons

2 tablespoons olive oil

4 garlic cloves, minced

2 tablespoons capers, drained

6 boneless, skinless chicken breasts

1 (14-ounce) can artichoke hearts, drained and rinsed

3 cups instant brown rice

1. In your slow cooker, combine the lemon juice, oil, garlic, and capers. Add the chicken and artichoke hearts.

2. Cover the slow cooker and cook on Low heat for 6 hours, or High heat for 2 hours.

3. Stir in the brown rice. Re-cover the cooker and let sit for 10 to 15 minutes until the rice is soft and fluffy.

4. Refrigerate individual portions in airtight containers for up to 4 days, or freeze for up to 4 months.

* **Prep Ahead:** Combine the lemon juice, oil, garlic, capers, artichoke hearts, and chicken in an airtight container. Refrigerate for up to 1 day, or freeze for up to 3 months. If you want to prep this recipe up to 4 days in advance and keep it in the refrigerator, keep the chicken breasts in their original packaging (refrigerating them in the acidic marinade for more than a day can make them tough). If frozen, thaw the ingredients in the refrigerator overnight before adding to your slow cooker.

* **Substitution Tip:** Instead of brown rice, spoon the chicken and sauce over Mashed Potatoes (page 143).

Per Serving: Calories: 328; Protein: 28g; Fat: 8g; Carbohydrates: 39g; Fiber: 4g; Sodium: 435mg

Chicken Parmesan with Zucchini Noodles

Serves 6 / Prep Time: 5 minutes / Cook Time: 6 hours (Low)

5-INGREDIENT   FREEZER-FRIENDLY   ONE-POT

Swap out traditional pasta for spiralized zucchini in this modern take on a classic Italian-American meal. "Zucchini noodles" are increasingly easy to find in the produce section of most major grocery stores. I prefer the fresh option to frozen zucchini noodles, which can get waterlogged and soggy. The "zoodles" don't require much cooking, so you can throw them into your slow cooker and let the hot sauce warm them.

4 cups Marinara Sauce (page 135), or jarred pasta sauce of choice

6 boneless, skinless chicken breasts

1 cup Italian-seasoned bread crumbs

1½ pounds spiralized zucchini

3 ounces fresh mozzarella, thinly sliced

1. Pour about 1 cup of marinara into the bottom of your slow cooker. Arrange the chicken breasts in a single layer. Spoon the bread crumbs over the chicken, gently pressing them onto the chicken to help them adhere. Pour in the remaining 3 cups of marinara.

2. Cover the slow cooker and cook on Low heat for 6 hours.

3. Stir in the zucchini noodles. Top the chicken with the mozzarella. Re-cover the slow cooker and cook for 3 to 4 minutes until the cheese melts.

4. Refrigerate individual portions in airtight containers for up to 4 days, or freeze for up to 4 months.

⊹ **Prep Ahead:** Place the chicken in a shallow airtight container in a single layer. Cover with the bread crumbs, gently pressing them onto the chicken to help them stick. Cover and refrigerate for up to 2 days. Measure the marinara, cheese, and zucchini noodles and refrigerate in separate containers.

⊹ **Ingredient Tip:** If using jarred sauce, choose one without added sugar. Rao's and Victoria are popular, but on a budget, Classico Tomato Basil sauce is also a great choice.

Per Serving: Calories: 247; Protein: 32g; Fat: 6g; Carbohydrates: 19g; Fiber: 4g; Sodium: 636mg

Persian-Inspired Chicken with Pomegranate

Serves 6 / Prep Time: 15 minutes / Cook Time: 8 hours (Low); 2 hours (High)

DAIRY-FREE   FREEZER-FRIENDLY

This recipe is inspired by a classic Persian stew known as *Fesenjan* that's often eaten on the longest night of the year to celebrate winter. Finely chopped walnuts and pomegranate juice come together in an earthy, juicy sauce flavored with warm spices. Bone-in chicken thighs add to the rich flavor of this dish, and the fresh pomegranate seeds sprinkled over the top add acidity and crunch.

1 tablespoon olive oil

2 onions, thinly sliced

1 teaspoon ground turmeric

½ teaspoon ground cinnamon

¼ teaspoon ground allspice

1 cup pomegranate juice

6 bone-in chicken thighs, skin removed

6 carrots, cut into coins

1 cup walnuts, finely chopped

1 teaspoon salt

½ cup whole-wheat couscous

¼ cup pomegranate seeds (optional)

1. In a skillet over medium heat, heat the oil. Add the onions and cook for 4 to 5 minutes until browned. Stir in the turmeric, cinnamon, and allspice and cook for 1 minute more until toasted and fragrant.

2. Pour in the pomegranate juice. Let simmer for 5 minutes until slightly reduced.

3. In your slow cooker, combine the chicken, carrots, walnuts, and salt. Pour the pomegranate sauce over the top.

4. Cover the slow cooker and cook on Low heat for 8 hours, or on High heat for 2 hours.

5. Stir in the couscous. Re-cover the cooker and cook on Low heat for 10 minutes, or until softened. Sprinkle the stew with pomegranate seeds (if using).

6. Refrigerate individual portions in airtight containers for up to 4 days, or freeze for up to 4 months.

* **Prep Ahead:** Prepare the ingredients as instructed in steps 1 and 2, adding them to an airtight container along with the carrots, walnuts, and salt. Store the chicken separately. Refrigerate for up to 2 days, or freeze for up to 4 months. If frozen, thaw the ingredients in the refrigerator overnight before adding to your slow cooker.
* **Substitution Tip:** This recipe is also tasty with quinoa instead of couscous. Increase the cooking time in step 5 to 20 minutes.

Per Serving: Calories: 475; Protein: 32g; Fat: 25g; Carbohydrates: 34g; Fiber: 6g; Sodium: 483mg

Buffalo Chicken–Stuffed Sweet Potatoes

Serves 6 / Prep Time: 5 minutes / Cook Time: 6 hours (Low)

5-INGREDIENT   FREEZER-FRIENDLY   GLUTEN-FREE   ONE-POT

Baked sweet potatoes are a great base for spicy shredded chicken and tangy blue cheese. Wrapping the potatoes in aluminum foil and placing them right on top of the chicken means you can cook everything at once. Be careful when you unwrap them. They'll be very hot and there may be water trapped in the foil—let that water drain away. I recommend using a Buffalo-style hot sauce like Frank's.

2 pounds boneless, skinless chicken breasts

1 cup hot sauce

6 sweet potatoes

¼ cup crumbled blue cheese

¼ cup fresh cilantro (optional)

1. In your slow cooker, combine the chicken and hot sauce. Wrap each sweet potato in foil and place them on top of the chicken.

2. Cover the slow cooker and cook on Low heat for 6 hours.

3. Carefully remove the sweet potatoes from the slow cooker.

4. Using two forks, shred the chicken in the sauce. Stir the chicken into the sauce and let sit for at least 10 minutes to soak up the flavor.

5. Cut open the sweet potatoes. Fill with shredded chicken and top with blue cheese crumbles and cilantro (if using).

6. If prepping ahead to reheat later, cut each sweet potato into 6 slices and place them into individual airtight containers. Top with chicken, blue cheese, and cilantro and refrigerate for up to 4 days. Slicing the sweet potatoes helps them reheat evenly as opposed to keeping them whole.

* **Prep Ahead:** Combine the chicken and hot sauce in an airtight container. Refrigerate for up to 2 days, or freeze for up to 4 months. Wrap the potatoes in foil and keep separate. If frozen, thaw the ingredients in the refrigerator overnight before adding to your slow cooker.
* **Ingredient Tip:** This recipe results in medium-spicy chicken. If you want to tone down the heat, stir in a few tablespoons of plain fat-free Greek yogurt.

Per Serving: Calories: 303; Protein: 34g; Fat: 5g; Carbohydrates: 32g; Fiber: 4g; Sodium: 1,015mg

Greek Stuffed Chicken Breasts

Serves 6 / Prep Time: 10 minutes / Cook Time: 6 hours (Low) plus 15 minutes (High)

Your kitchen will smell so good after this recipe cooks all day. Stuffing boneless chicken breasts with a combination of artichoke hearts, spinach, and feta cheese helps keep them tender and gives them a ton of flavor. For best results, use thick chicken breasts, not thin cutlets, which are difficult to stuff and will overcook in the slow cooker.

6 boneless, skinless
   chicken breasts
6 canned artichoke
   hearts, chopped
2 cups fresh baby
   spinach, chopped
1 red bell pepper, seeded
   and diced
¼ cup crumbled
   feta cheese
2 teaspoons dried oregano
½ teaspoon freshly
   ground black pepper
1½ cups whole-wheat
   couscous
¼ cup pitted Kalamata
   olives, chopped

1. Using a sharp knife, cut a deep pocket in each chicken breast, being careful not to split the breast completely through.

2. In a small bowl, stir together the artichokes, spinach, red bell pepper, and feta. Stuff the mixture into each chicken breast. Place the breasts, cut-side up, in your slow cooker and season with oregano and pepper.

3. Cover the slow cooker and cook on Low heat for 6 hours.

4. Stir in the couscous and olives. If the mixture looks dry, add ¼ cup of water. Cover and cook on High heat for 10 to 15 minutes, or until cooked through.

5. Refrigerate individual portions in airtight containers for up to 4 days.

   ✳ **Prep Ahead:** Stuff the chicken breasts as described in steps 1 and 2. Transfer to an airtight container and refrigerate for up to 2 days.

   ✳ **Cooking Tip:** The stuffed chicken breasts will release a significant amount of liquid, even though you add them to a dry slow cooker. There should be enough to cook the couscous, but if it looks dry after mixing it in, add a bit of water or broth.

Per Serving: Calories: 374; Protein: 33g; Fat: 6g; Carbohydrates: 51g; Fiber: 9g; Sodium: 460mg

Thai Peanut Chicken with Cauliflower Rice

Serves 6 / **Prep Time: 10 minutes** / **Cook Time: 6 hours (Low)**

DAIRY-FREE FREEZER-FRIENDLY ONE-POT

Chicken breasts cooked in a rich, creamy peanut sauce creates a tasty dish I never tire of. Look for natural peanut butter without any added sugar or oils. If you can't eat peanuts, sunflower seed butter makes a great substitute.

1 (14-ounce) can
  coconut milk
½ cup natural
  peanut butter
2 tablespoons low-sodium
  soy sauce
2 tablespoons rice
  wine vinegar
6 garlic cloves, minced
2 tablespoons minced
  peeled fresh ginger
6 boneless, skinless
  chicken breasts
2 tablespoons cornstarch
Juice of 1 lime
2 cups cauliflower rice
Chopped scallion, for
  garnish (optional)

1. In your slow cooker, whisk the coconut milk, peanut butter, soy sauce, vinegar, garlic, and ginger until smooth. Add the chicken and turn to coat.

2. Cover the slow cooker and cook on Low heat for 6 hours.

3. Whisk in the cornstarch and lime juice. Add the cauliflower rice. Let sit for 5 to 10 minutes until the sauce thickens and the cauliflower rice is soft.

4. Garnish with scallion (if using). Refrigerate individual portions in airtight containers for up to 4 days, or freeze for up to 4 months.

Prep Ahead: In an airtight container, combine the coconut milk, peanut butter, soy sauce, vinegar, garlic, and ginger. Add the chicken and turn to coat. Refrigerate for up to 2 days, or freeze for up to 4 months. If frozen, thaw the ingredients in the refrigerator overnight before adding to your slow cooker.

Per Serving: Calories: 397; Protein: 31g; Fat: 25g; Carbohydrates: 11g; Fiber: 2g; Sodium: 438mg

Cranberry-Glazed Turkey Tenderloin with Wild Rice

Serves 6 / Prep Time: 10 minutes / Cook Time: 6 to 8 hours (Low); 3 to 4 hours (High)

DAIRY-FREE   FREEZER-FRIENDLY   GLUTEN-FREE

This dish is like a mini Thanksgiving dinner. The wild rice has all my favorite stuffing ingredients mixed in, but the celery is what gives it that classic stuffing flavor. Look for canned chipotle peppers in adobo in the international section of your grocery store.

1½ cups wild rice

3 carrots, diced

3 celery stalks, sliced

6 ounces cremini mushrooms, sliced

½ onion, diced

1 teaspoon poultry seasoning

3 cups Chicken Stock (page 132), or low-sodium chicken broth

1 cup cranberry sauce

¼ cup sugar-free ketchup

1 canned chipotle pepper in adobo sauce, minced

1½ pounds turkey tenderloin

1. In your slow cooker, combine the wild rice, carrots, celery, mushrooms, onion, and poultry seasoning. Stir in the chicken stock.

2. In a small bowl, whisk the cranberry sauce, ketchup, and chipotle to combine. Brush the glaze onto the turkey. Place the glazed turkey tenderloin into the slow cooker.

3. Cover the slow cooker and cook on Low heat for 6 to 8 hours, or High heat for 3 to 4 hours, or until the wild rice is tender and the turkey is cooked through and reaches an internal temperature of 165°F.

4. Refrigerate individual portions in airtight containers for up to 4 days, or freeze for up to 4 months.

☀ **Prep Ahead:** Combine the rice and vegetables in an airtight container; pour the broth into a separate container. Glaze the turkey as described in step 2 and place it into a third container. Refrigerate for up to 2 days, or freeze for up to 4 months. If frozen, thaw the ingredients in the refrigerator overnight before adding to your slow cooker.

☀ **Substitution Tip:** Try this recipe with turkey breast cutlets or pork tenderloin.

Per Serving: Calories: 413; Protein: 30g; Fat: 4g; Carbohydrates: 64g; Fiber: 4g; Sodium: 735mg

Cilantro-Lime Chicken with Black Beans and Corn

Serves 6 / **Prep Time: 15 minutes** / **Cook Time: 8 hours (Low); 3 hours (High)**

DAIRY-FREE   FREEZER-FRIENDLY   GLUTEN-FREE

This flavorful combination of chicken, black beans, and corn is delicious on its own, but I also love using it as a base for other recipes. Add it to chicken broth with a minced chipotle pepper for a quick soup, or turn it into tacos by wrapping it in corn tortillas. Searing the chicken in step 1 gives it extra flavor, but you can skip that step if you're in a rush.

1 tablespoon olive oil

1½ pounds boneless, skinless chicken thighs

1 (15.5-ounce) can low-sodium black beans, drained and rinsed

5 garlic cloves, minced

2 teaspoons chili powder

Grated zest of 2 limes

Juice of 2 limes

½ teaspoon kosher salt

2 cups frozen corn

¼ cup fresh cilantro, chopped

1. In a skillet over medium-high heat, heat the oil. Add the chicken and cook for 5 to 7 minutes per side until browned.

2. In your slow cooker, combine the black beans, garlic, chili powder, lime zest, lime juice, and salt. Arrange the chicken thighs on top.

3. Cover the slow cooker and cook on Low heat for 8 hours, or High heat for 3 hours.

4. Transfer the chicken to a cutting board. Cut it into ½-inch cubes and return to the pot.

5. Stir in the corn and cilantro. Re-cover the cooker and cook on High heat for 5 to 10 minutes, or until heated through.

6. Refrigerate individual portions in airtight containers for up to 4 days, or freeze for up to 4 months.

‣ **Prep Ahead:** Brown the chicken as instructed in step 1, transferring it to an airtight container. In a second container, combine the beans, garlic, chili powder, lime zest, lime juice, and salt. Refrigerate for up to 2 days, or freeze for up to 4 months. If frozen, thaw the ingredients in the refrigerator overnight before adding to your slow cooker.

Per Serving: Calories: 279; Protein: 22g; Fat: 11g; Carbohydrates: 25g; Fiber: 6g; Sodium: 439mg

Cashew Chicken

Serves 6 / Prep Time: 5 minutes / Cook Time: 8 hours (Low)

DAIRY-FREE   FREEZER-FRIENDLY   ONE-POT

This cashew chicken is even better than takeout. Bone-in chicken thighs stay really juicy, and the salty, tangy sauce is flavorful. You can eat this chicken on its own or pair it with instant rice or a cooked whole grain—I love it over farro!

⅓ cup low-sodium
  soy sauce

¼ cup rice vinegar

2 tablespoons chili paste

3 garlic cloves, minced

1 tablespoon grated
  peeled fresh ginger

½ teaspoon freshly
  ground black pepper

6 bone-in chicken thighs,
  skin removed

2 bell peppers, any color,
  seeded and sliced

1 cup raw
  unsalted cashews

1. In your slow cooker, whisk the soy sauce, vinegar, chili paste, garlic, ginger, and pepper to combine. Add the chicken thighs, turning them to coat. Top with the bell peppers and cashews.

2. Cover the slow cooker and cook on Low heat for 8 hours.

3. Refrigerate individual portions in airtight containers for up to 4 days, or freeze for up to 4 months.

❋ **Prep Ahead:** Prepare the sauce as described in step 1, adding it to an airtight container. Add the chicken, bell peppers, and cashews. Refrigerate for up to 2 days, or freeze for up to 4 months. If frozen, thaw the ingredients in the refrigerator overnight before adding to your slow cooker.

❋ **Ingredient Tip:** Bone-in thighs have more flavor and stay juicier during long cook times than boneless thighs, but the skin can make your recipe greasy. Pull off the skin before adding the chicken to your slow cooker for the best of both worlds.

Per Serving: Calories: 284; Protein: 27g; Fat: 15g; Carbohydrates: 12g; Fiber: 2g; Sodium: 696mg

Apricot Chicken with Couscous

Serves 6 / Prep Time: 6 minutes / Cook Time: 6 hours (Low)

DAIRY-FREE   FREEZER-FRIENDLY   ONE-POT

Dried apricots and balsamic vinegar give this chicken a sweet, tangy flavor that will have you begging for more. The apricots plump and soften as they cook but retain some of their chewy texture. I like to serve this recipe with nutty whole-wheat couscous to balance the sweet flavors. If you have extra apricots after making this, they're delicious chopped and stirred into Cherry-Almond Granola (page 20).

¼ cup Chicken
  Stock (page 132),
  or low-sodium
  chicken broth
2 tablespoons
  balsamic vinegar
2 tablespoons honey
1 shallot, thickly sliced
1 tablespoon fresh
  thyme leaves
6 boneless, skinless
  chicken breasts
3 ounces dried apricots
1 cup whole-wheat
  couscous

1. In your slow cooker, stir together the chicken stock, vinegar, honey, shallot, and thyme. Add the chicken breasts and apricots.

2. Cover the slow cooker and cook on Low heat for 6 hours.

3. Stir in the couscous. Re-cover the cooker and cook on Low heat for 5 to 10 minutes more until the couscous is soft and cooked through.

4. Refrigerate individual portions in airtight containers for up to 4 days, or freeze for up to 4 months.

❋ **Prep Ahead:** Prepare the sauce as described in step 1, adding it to an airtight container. Add the chicken and apricots and refrigerate for up to 2 days, or freeze for up to 4 months. Measure the couscous and store it in a separate container. If frozen, thaw the ingredients in the refrigerator overnight before adding to your slow cooker.

❋ **Ingredient Tip:** It only takes about 6 hours to cook chicken breasts, but they'll stay juicy for a few more hours if your slow cooker switches over to "keep warm." If you want a longer cooking time, substitute boneless, skinless chicken thighs for the chicken breasts and set your timer to 8 hours in step 2.

Per Serving: Calories: 282; Protein: 28g; Fat: 3g; Carbohydrates: 38g; Fiber: 5g; Sodium: 189mg

Herby Chicken and Potatoes

Serves 6 / Prep Time: 10 minutes / Cook Time: 8 hours (Low); 3 hours (High)

DAIRY-FREE · FREEZER-FRIENDLY · GLUTEN-FREE

Roasted chicken is one of my absolute favorite dinners, but I hate having to stay home while it's in the oven. This recipe has that classic roast chicken vibe, but making it in the slow cooker means it doesn't require so much attention. Because the chicken skin doesn't crisp up in the slow cooker, and crispy is the way I prefer it, I pull it off and throw it away before adding the chicken to the slow cooker. This also makes the meal less greasy and lower in saturated fat.

1½ pounds small red potatoes, quartered

1 tablespoon olive oil

1 teaspoon garlic powder

1 teaspoon paprika

1 teaspoon dried thyme

½ teaspoon dried crushed rosemary

½ teaspoon kosher salt

½ teaspoon freshly ground black pepper

6 bone-in chicken thighs, skin removed

1 pound fresh green beans, trimmed

1 lemon, cut into 6 wedges

1. In your slow cooker, stir together potatoes and oil to coat the potatoes well.

2. In a small bowl, stir together the garlic powder, paprika, thyme, rosemary, salt, and pepper. Rub the spice mixture onto the chicken thighs. Arrange the chicken in a single layer over the potatoes.

3. Wrap the slow cooker lid with a clean kitchen towel to trap condensation and cover the slow cooker with it. Cook on Low heat for 8 hours, or High heat for 3 hours.

4. Add the green beans. Re-cover the cooker and cook on High heat for 10 to 15 minutes, or until cooked.

5. Refrigerate individual portions in airtight containers, with a lemon wedge for squeezing, for up to 4 days, or freeze for up to 4 months.

✦ **Prep Ahead:** Drizzle the potatoes with oil and place them in an airtight container. Season the chicken breasts as instructed in step 2 and place them in a second container. Measure the green beans and lemon wedges into a third container. Refrigerate for up to 2 days.

✦ **Substitution Tip:** Substitute your favorite roast chicken rub for the individual spices.

Per Serving: Calories: 268; Protein: 28g; Fat: 12g; Carbohydrates: 15g; Fiber: 5g; Sodium: 258mg

Chicken and Shrimp Jambalaya

**Serves 6 / Prep Time: 5 minutes / Cook Time: 6 hours (Low) plus 15 minutes (High);
3 hours plus 15 minutes (High)**

DAIRY-FREE FREEZER-FRIENDLY GLUTEN-FREE ONE-POT

When I was younger, boxed jambalaya made an appearance on my family's dinner table on a weekly basis. It was delicious, but it was also full of sodium and preservatives—I knew I could make something healthier and just as delicious from scratch. This is the slow cooker version of one of my go-to recipes. I like to mix things up using both chicken and shrimp, but use one or the other if you'd rather keep things simple.

3 celery stalks, chopped

1 onion, diced

1 bell pepper, any color, seeded and diced

1 (28-ounce) can diced fire-roasted tomatoes, drained

4 garlic cloves, minced

1 tablespoon dried oregano

1 tablespoon Cajun seasoning

¼ teaspoon cayenne pepper (optional)

1 pound boneless, skinless chicken breasts

1 pound cooked shrimp, tails removed

2 cups instant brown rice

1. In your slow cooker, stir together the celery, onion, bell pepper, tomatoes, garlic, oregano, Cajun seasoning, and cayenne. Add the chicken.

2. Cover the slow cooker and cook on Low heat for 6 hours, or High heat for 3 hours. Keep warm until ready to eat.

3. Transfer the chicken to a cutting board and dice or shred, then return it to the cooker.

4. Stir in the shrimp and brown rice. Re-cover the cooker and cook on High heat for 10 to 15 minutes, or until the rice is soft and fluffy.

5. Refrigerate individual portions in airtight containers for up to 4 days, or freeze for up to 4 months.

✳ **Prep Ahead:** Combine the celery, onion, bell pepper, tomatoes, garlic, oregano, Cajun seasoning, cayenne, and chicken in an airtight container. Refrigerate for up to 2 days. Refrigerate the shrimp in a separate container for up to 4 days.

Per Serving: Calories: 291; Protein: 34g; Fat: 3g; Carbohydrates: 34g; Fiber: 6g; Sodium: 765mg

Maple-Mustard Drumsticks

Serves 6 / **Prep Time: 5 minutes** / **Cook Time: 8 hours (Low); 4 hours (High)**

DAIRY-FREE FREEZER-FRIENDLY GLUTEN-FREE ONE-POT

These chicken drumsticks are inspired by one of my favorite wing sauces. They're sweet and tangy, with the tiniest bit of heat. Chicken skin doesn't come out well in the slow cooker, so pull it off before coating the drumsticks in the sauce. If you have kitchen shears, now's the time to put them to work—they make removing the skin much easier. If you don't have shears, a sharp paring knife also works.

6 chicken drumsticks, skin removed

¼ cup pure maple syrup

½ cup Dijon mustard

2 tablespoons hot sauce

1½ pounds small yellow potatoes

6 carrots, cut into 1-inch pieces

½ teaspoon sea salt

½ teaspoon freshly ground black pepper

1. Place the chicken in your slow cooker. Pour in the maple syrup, Dijon, and hot sauce. Stir well to thoroughly coat the chicken.

2. Add the potatoes and carrots.

3. Wrap the slow cooker lid with a clean kitchen towel to trap condensation and cover the slow cooker with it. Cook on Low heat for 8 hours, or High heat for 4 hours.

4. Season with salt and pepper.

5. Refrigerate individual portions in airtight containers for up to 4 days, or freeze for up to 4 months.

✳ **Prep Ahead:** In an airtight container, combine the maple syrup, Dijon, and hot sauce. Add the chicken and turn to coat. Add the potatoes and carrots. Refrigerate for up to 2 days.

✳ **Cooking Tip:** The ingredients in this recipe give off a lot of liquid as they cook. Placing a kitchen towel under the slow cooker lid traps condensation to keep your recipe from coming out soupy.

Per Serving: Calories: 238; Protein: 17g; Fat: 2g; Carbohydrates: 36g; Fiber: 4g; Sodium: 872mg

Turkey Swedish Meatballs

Serves 6 / **Prep Time: 15 minutes** / **Cook Time: 8 hours (Low)**

FREEZER-FRIENDLY

This is one of my absolute favorite recipes to make in my slow cooker. Wrapping the potatoes in aluminum foil lets you cook them at the same time as the meatballs, while keeping them out of the sauce. You can eat them plain with a little salt and pepper, or gently mash them and serve the meatballs and gravy over the top.

1 cup panko bread crumbs

½ cup milk

1 teaspoon
granulated onion

2 large eggs

1 teaspoon salt

¼ teaspoon
ground nutmeg

2 pounds lean
ground turkey

1 cup Beef Bone
Broth (page 133), or
low-sodium beef broth

1 tablespoon
Worcestershire sauce

1½ pounds baby potatoes

3 tablespoons light
sour cream

1. In a large bowl, combine the panko, milk, and granulated onion. Let sit for 5 minutes.

2. Add the eggs, salt, nutmeg, and ground turkey. With damp hands, mix to combine and form the turkey mixture into 24 meatballs.

3. In your slow cooker, combine the beef bone broth and Worcestershire sauce. Add the meatballs. Wrap the potatoes in a large piece of foil and place the packet in the slow cooker.

4. Cover the slow cooker and cook on Low heat for 8 hours.

5. Carefully remove the potato packet. Stir the sour cream into the meatballs.

6. Refrigerate individual portions in airtight containers for up to 4 days, or freeze for up to 4 months.

- **Prep Ahead:** Prepare the meatballs as instructed in steps 1 and 2 and place in an airtight container. Combine the broth and Worcestershire sauce in a separate container or jar. Refrigerate for up to 2 days, or freeze for up to 6 months. If frozen, thaw the ingredients in the refrigerator overnight before adding to your slow cooker.
- **Ingredient Tip:** Ground turkey is great for making Swedish meatballs. It has a darker, meatier flavor than ground chicken but is still mild enough to let the delicate flavors of the nutmeg and cream shine through.

Per Serving: Calories: 402; Protein: 37g; Fat: 14g; Carbohydrates: 35g; Fiber: 3g; Sodium: 608mg

Pork, Lamb, and Beef

Tacos al Pastor

Serves 8 / Prep Time: 10 minutes / Cook Time: 8 hours (Low); 4 hours (High)

DAIRY-FREE FREEZER-FRIENDLY GLUTEN-FREE ONE-POT

Tacos al pastor is one of my favorite things to order when we go out for Mexican food, but I also love making this dish at home in my slow cooker. These tacos are delicious with just the pork and chopped pineapple, but it's also a great opportunity to clean out your refrigerator and see what other toppings you can find. Some of my favorites are fresh cilantro, sliced radishes, shredded cabbage, and pickled jalapeños.

½ cup Chicken
  Stock (page 132),
  or low-sodium
  chicken broth
¼ cup apple cider vinegar
2 pounds boneless pork
  shoulder (picnic roast),
  trimmed and cut into
  2-inch cubes
4 canned chipotle
  peppers in adobo sauce,
  finely chopped
1 red onion, thinly sliced
1 pound fresh
  pineapple, sliced
24 corn tortillas

1. In your slow cooker, combine the chicken stock and vinegar.

2. Rub the pork with the chipotles and place it in the slow cooker. Cover the pork with the red onion. Arrange the pineapple on top.

3. Cover the slow cooker and cook on Low heat for 8 hours, or High heat for 4 hours.

4. Transfer the pork and pineapple to a cutting board. Using two forks, shred the pork. Chop the pineapple. Return the pork and pineapple to the cooker and stir to combine with the sauce.

5. Refrigerate individual portions in airtight containers for up to 4 days, or freeze for up to 4 months. Serve the pork in the tortillas.

  ✳ **Prep Ahead:** Trim and cube the pork as instructed, rub with the chipotles in adobo sauce, and place in an airtight container. Pour in the chicken stock and vinegar. Store the red onion and pineapple in a separate container. Refrigerate for up to 5 days, or freeze for up to 4 months. If frozen, thaw the ingredients in the refrigerator overnight before adding to your slow cooker.

  ✳ **Ingredient Tip:** Arranging the pineapple on top of the pork means the juices run down through it while it cooks, infusing it with flavor and keeping it moist.

Per Serving: Calories: 432; Protein: 35g; Fat: 13g; Carbohydrates: 45g; Fiber: 6g; Sodium: 241mg

Pork with Pears

Serves 6 / Prep Time: 15 minutes / Cook Time: 8 hours plus 10 minutes (Low);
4 hours plus 10 minutes (High)

FREEZER-FRIENDLY   GLUTEN-FREE

Pork and pears are a classic combination that always reminds me of fall. In this recipe, shallot, garlic, and fresh thyme balance the sweetness of the pears and the cider-based gravy. Be sure to buy pork tenderloin, which is different from pork loin. Thanks to the pears, this recipe is enough to stand on its own as a meal. If you want a side dish, Braised Collard Greens (page 137) and Ratatouille (page 136) are great options.

1 tablespoon olive oil
2 pounds pork tenderloin
6 pears, quartered
   and cored
4 garlic cloves, peeled
2 shallots, chopped
1 tablespoon fresh
   thyme leaves
½ cup apple cider
½ teaspoon kosher salt
½ teaspoon freshly
   ground black pepper
2 tablespoons heavy
   (whipping) cream
1 tablespoon cornstarch

1. In a large skillet over medium-high heat, heat the oil. Add the pork tenderloin and cook for 5 minutes per side until browned. Transfer the seared pork to your slow cooker. Arrange the pears around the pork and add the garlic, shallots, thyme, cider, salt, and pepper.

2. Cover the slow cooker and cook on Low heat for 8 hours, or High heat for 4 hours.

3. Whisk in the heavy cream and cornstarch and cook for 5 to 10 minutes more to thicken the sauce.

4. Refrigerate individual portions in airtight containers for up to 4 days, or freeze for up to 4 months.

✣ **Prep Ahead:** Sear the pork as instructed in step 1 and transfer it to an airtight container. In a second container, combine the pears, garlic, shallots, thyme, cider, salt, and pepper. Refrigerate for up to 5 days. Add the cream and cornstarch when cooking, as instructed.

Per Serving: Calories: 445; Protein: 45g; Fat: 17g; Carbohydrates: 27g; Fiber: 4g; Sodium: 285mg

Pork Chops with Parsnips

Serves 6 / Prep Time: 5 minutes / Cook Time: 6 hours (Low)

DAIRY-FREE FREEZER-FRIENDLY GLUTEN-FREE ONE-POT

Lemon zest, rosemary, and garlic give these pork chops a bright, summery vibe. Look for bone-in pork chops that are at least ½ inch thick to help prevent them from cooking too quickly and drying out. If you can only find thin-cut chops, or if you don't like cooking with bones, use a boneless pork tenderloin.

⅓ cup Chicken Stock (page 132), or Vegetable Broth (page 134), or low-sodium store-bought broth
Grated zest of 2 lemons
Juice of 2 lemons
1 teaspoon dried crushed rosemary
2 garlic cloves, sliced
½ teaspoon red pepper flakes (optional)
8 parsnips, cut into coins
8 carrots, cut into coins
1 red onion, sliced
6 bone-in pork chops
½ teaspoon kosher salt
¼ teaspoon freshly ground black pepper
2 tablespoons cornstarch

1. In your slow cooker, whisk the chicken stock, lemon zest, lemon juice, rosemary, garlic, and red pepper flakes (if using) to combine.

2. Add the parsnips, carrots, and red onion. Place the pork chops on top and season with salt and pepper.

3. Cover the slow cooker and cook on Low heat for 6 hours, or until the pork chops reach an internal temperature of 145°F.

4. Remove the pork chops from the slow cooker. Whisk in the cornstarch and let sit for 5 minutes until the gravy is slightly thickened.

5. Refrigerate individual portions in airtight containers for up to 4 days, or freeze for up to 4 months.

✳ **Prep Ahead:** Combine the pork chops, chicken stock, lemon zest and juice, rosemary, garlic, red pepper flakes (if using), parsnips, carrots, and red onion in an airtight container. Refrigerate for up to 3 days, or freeze for up to 3 months. If frozen, thaw the ingredients in the refrigerator overnight before adding to your slow cooker.

Per Serving: Calories: 345; Protein: 21g; Fat: 8g; Carbohydrates: 50g; Fiber: 10g; Sodium: 681mg

Roast Pork with Mashed Potatoes

Serves 8 / **Prep Time: 10 minutes** / **Cook Time: 8 hours (Low)**

FREEZER-FRIENDLY GLUTEN-FREE

The pork in this recipe is inspired by pernil, a garlicky, slow-roasted pork traditionally served in Latin American countries at Christmastime. If you ask me, it's way too delicious to be saved for just once a year. To adapt this recipe for the slow cooker, I swapped the traditional bone-in pork shoulder for a leaner pork roast. It's delicious served with mashed potatoes and a big green salad.

6 garlic cloves, minced

1 tablespoon
   dried oregano

1½ tablespoons olive oil

1½ tablespoons
   white vinegar

¼ teaspoon salt

¼ teaspoon freshly
   ground black pepper

1 (3-pound) pork roast

1 pound small red
   potatoes, quartered

1 tablespoon butter

½ cup plain fat-free
   Greek yogurt

1. In a small bowl, stir together the garlic, oregano, oil, vinegar, salt, and pepper. Rub the spice mixture all over the pork and place the pork in your slow cooker.

2. Wrap the potatoes in a large piece of aluminum foil and place the packet into the slow cooker.

3. Cover the slow cooker and cook on Low heat for 8 hours, or until the pork is tender.

4. Carefully unwrap the potatoes and transfer to a large bowl. Add the butter and yogurt. Using a potato masher or heavy wooden spoon, mash the potatoes to your desired consistency.

5. Refrigerate individual portions in airtight containers for up to 4 days, or freeze for up to 4 months.

   ❋ **Prep Ahead:** Prepare the pork as instructed in step 1, placing it in an airtight container. Cut the potatoes, place them into a second container, and cover with water. Refrigerate for up to 5 days. Drain the potatoes before cooking.

   ❋ **Cooking Tip:** The pork will release a significant amount of liquid as it cooks. Wrapping the potatoes in a foil packet keeps them dry and out of the fat.

Per Serving: Calories: 283; Protein: 31g; Fat: 12g; Carbohydrates: 11g; Fiber: 2g; Sodium: 533mg

Maple Baked Beans with Pork Tenderloin

Serves 6 / Prep Time: 5 minutes / Cook Time: 8 hours (Low)

DAIRY-FREE FREEZER-FRIENDLY GLUTEN-FREE ONE-POT

Whole pork tenderloin stays surprisingly juicy in a slow cooker, even when cooked all day. In this recipe, it's complemented by my favorite "baked" beans. They have a great balance of sweet, smoky, and tangy flavors and a firm but creamy texture. Pair with a side salad, Braised Collard Greens (page 137), or green beans to round out the meal.

2 (15-ounce) cans low-sodium pinto beans, drained and rinsed

1 red onion, chopped

2 tablespoons apple cider vinegar

2 tablespoons pure maple syrup

1 teaspoon smoked paprika

1 (1½- to 2-pound) pork tenderloin

½ teaspoon kosher salt

½ teaspoon freshly ground black pepper

1. In your slow cooker, combine the pinto beans, red onion, vinegar, maple syrup, and paprika.

2. Season the pork with salt and pepper, then nestle it into the beans.

3. Cover the slow cooker and cook on Low heat for 8 hours.

4. Refrigerate individual portions in airtight containers for up to 4 days, or freeze for up to 4 months.

✤ **Prep Ahead:** In an airtight container, combine the beans, red onion, vinegar, maple syrup, and paprika. Season the pork and store it in a second container. Refrigerate for up to 5 days, or freeze for up to 6 months. If frozen, thaw the ingredients in the refrigerator overnight before adding to your slow cooker.

✤ **Ingredient Tip:** Using smoked paprika instead of traditional paprika gives the beans a subtle barbecue flavor. Use traditional paprika, if you prefer.

Per Serving: Calories: 382; Protein: 42g; Fat: 9g; Carbohydrates: 30g; Fiber: 11g; Sodium: 317mg

Lamb and Potato Curry

Serves 6 / Prep Time: 15 minutes / Cook Time: 8 hours (Low)

DAIRY-FREE FREEZER-FRIENDLY GLUTEN-FREE

Fire-roasted tomatoes and garam masala—a spicy curry powder made with toasted spices such as cinnamon, cardamom, and peppercorns—give this lamb curry so much flavor. Browning the lamb before adding it to your slow cooker gives it a richer dimension and helps cook off some of the fat, so don't be tempted to skip this step.

1 tablespoon olive oil

2 pounds lamb stew meat, cubed

½ teaspoon kosher salt

1 (14.5-ounce) can fire-roasted diced tomatoes

1 onion, chopped

2 tablespoons garam masala

1 tablespoon grated peeled fresh ginger

1 pound fingerling potatoes

¼ cup canned coconut milk

2 cups frozen peas

2 tablespoons chopped fresh cilantro (optional)

1. In a large skillet over medium-high heat, heat the oil. Add the lamb in a single layer and sprinkle with salt. Cook for 3 to 4 minutes per side until deeply browned. Transfer the lamb to your slow cooker.

2. Add the tomatoes, onion, garam masala, and ginger. Stir in the potatoes.

3. Cover the slow cooker and cook on Low heat for 8 hours.

4. Stir in the coconut milk and peas. Re-cover the cooker and let sit for 2 to 3 minutes until warm. Top with cilantro (if using).

5. Refrigerate individual portions in airtight containers for up to 4 days, or freeze for up to 4 months.

Prep Ahead: Brown the lamb as instructed in step 1 and transfer it to an airtight container. Stir in the tomatoes, onion, garam masala, ginger, and potatoes. Refrigerate for up to 5 days, or freeze for up to 6 months. If frozen, thaw the ingredients in the refrigerator overnight before adding to your slow cooker.

Substitution Tip: If you don't want to open a can of coconut milk for just ¼ cup, use heavy (whipping) cream or half-and-half.

Per Serving: Calories: 360; Protein: 36g; Fat: 13g; Carbohydrates: 25g; Fiber: 6g; Sodium: 550mg

Pork with Sauerkraut

Serves 8 / Prep Time: 15 minutes / Cook Time: 8 hours (Low); 3 hours (High)

5-INGREDIENT   DAIRY-FREE   FREEZER-FRIENDLY   GLUTEN-FREE

This recipe takes me straight back to the German festivals I used to go to with my grandparents when I was a kid. Look for refrigerated or jarred sauerkraut instead of canned—it typically has a crisp texture closer to raw cabbage and won't get as mushy in the slow cooker. The long cooking time mellows the sauerkraut's pungent flavor, and an apple cooked along with it adds a touch of sweetness.

2 pounds pork tenderloin

½ teaspoon kosher salt

½ teaspoon freshly ground black pepper

1 tablespoon olive oil

1½ pounds fresh sauerkraut, drained

2 cups water

1 apple, thinly sliced

2 tablespoons caraway seeds (optional)

1. Season the pork all over with salt and pepper.

2. In a large skillet over medium-high heat, heat the oil. Add the pork and cook for 10 minutes, turning, until browned on all sides.

3. In your slow cooker, combine the sauerkraut, water, apple, and caraway seeds (if using). Add the pork.

4. Cover the slow cooker and cook on Low heat for 8 hours, or High heat for 3 hours.

5. Refrigerate individual portions in airtight containers for up to 4 days, or freeze for up to 4 months.

❋ **Prep Ahead:** Season and sear the pork loin as described in steps 1 and 2. Transfer to an airtight container. Measure the sauerkraut, water, apple, and caraway seeds (if using) into a second container. Refrigerate for up to 5 days.

❋ **Cooking Tip:** Searing the pork in a hot pan creates a crust that helps trap the juices inside and gives this dish a little more texture.

Per Serving: Calories: 268; Protein: 34g; Fat: 11g; Carbohydrates: 6g; Fiber: 3g; Sodium: 770mg

Picadillo-Stuffed Acorn Squash

Serves 6 / Prep Time: 15 minutes / Cook Time: 6 to 8 hours (Low); 3 hours (High)

DAIRY-FREE   FREEZER-FRIENDLY

Picadillo is a traditional Cuban recipe made with ground beef, peppers, and spices and cooked in a rich tomato sauce. It's similar to chili, but the addition of olives and raisins gives it a sweet, salty twist. Picadillo is traditionally served with rice and beans, but it also makes an excellent filling for stuffed Winter Squash (page 139).

1 tablespoon olive oil

2 pounds lean
   ground beef

1 small onion, diced

2 garlic cloves, minced

1 green bell pepper,
   seeded and chopped

½ cup pitted green olives,
   drained, chopped

1 (8-ounce) can
   tomato sauce

¼ cup raisins

1 tablespoon
   Worcestershire sauce

1 teaspoon ground cumin

¼ teaspoon salt

3 acorn squash, halved,
   seeds and pulp removed

1. In a large skillet over medium-high heat, heat the oil. Add the ground beef and cook for 5 to 8 minutes, stirring to break up the meat, until browned.

2. Add the onion and garlic. Cook for 3 to 4 minutes until softened. Stir in the green bell pepper, olives, tomato sauce, raisins, Worcestershire sauce, cumin, and salt. Transfer the picadillo to your slow cooker.

3. Place the acorn squash halves on top, staggering and stacking as needed to fit.

4. Cover the slow cooker and cook on Low heat for 6 to 8 hours, or High heat for 3 hours.

5. Remove the acorn squash. Spoon the picadillo into the squash halves.

6. Refrigerate individual portions in airtight containers for up to 4 days, or freeze for up to 4 months.

✢ **Prep Ahead:** Prepare the picadillo as described in steps 1 and 2, transferring it to an airtight container. Refrigerate for up to 2 days, or freeze for up to 6 months. If frozen, thaw the ingredients in the refrigerator overnight before adding to your slow cooker with the acorn squash.

Per Serving: Calories: 434; Protein: 34g; Fat: 19g; Carbohydrates: 35g; Fiber: 5g; Sodium: 614mg

Vietnamese-Inspired Rice Bowls

Serves 6 / **Prep Time: 5 minutes** / **Cook Time: 8 hours (Low)**

DAIRY-FREE FREEZER-FRIENDLY ONE-POT

These brown rice bowls are inspired by my favorite order at one of my favorite lunch places. The steak cooks in a rich and flavorful broth that also flavors the rice. Fresh herbs and vegetables piled on top provide balance and keep the flavors bright. An optional squeeze of fresh lime juice over the top brings the flavors together and adds a touch of acidity that cuts through the richness.

1 tablespoon sesame oil

2 shallots, sliced

4 garlic cloves, minced

3 tablespoons fish sauce

1 tablespoon low-sodium soy sauce

1 tablespoon sriracha

1 teaspoon pure maple syrup

1½ pounds flank steak, trimmed

1½ cups instant brown rice

1 cucumber, chopped

1 carrot, shredded

¼ cup fresh cilantro, chopped

Lime wedges, for serving (optional)

1. In your slow cooker, combine the oil, shallots, garlic, fish sauce, soy sauce, sriracha, and maple syrup. Add the steak and turn to coat.

2. Cover the slow cooker and cook on Low heat for 8 hours.

3. Transfer the beef to a cutting board and shred it. Return it to the slow cooker.

4. Stir the rice into the pot, re-cover the cooker, and cook on Low heat for 10 minutes until the rice is soft and fluffy.

5. Refrigerate individual portions of the rice, topped with shredded beef, cucumber, carrot, cilantro, and a lime wedge (if using), in airtight containers for up to 4 days. The rice and beef can also be frozen for up to 3 months.

☀ **Prep Ahead:** Place the steak in an airtight container and cover it with the oil, shallots, garlic, fish sauce, soy sauce, sriracha, and maple syrup. Refrigerate for up to 5 days, or freeze for up to 6 months. If frozen, thaw the ingredients in the refrigerator overnight before adding to your slow cooker.

Per Serving: Calories: 296; Protein: 26g; Fat: 11g; Carbohydrates: 23g; Fiber: 2g; Sodium: 913mg

Peach Barbecue Pulled Pork

Serves 6 / Prep Time: 10 minutes / Cook Time: 8 hours (Low)

DAIRY-FREE FREEZER-FRIENDLY

Barbecue pulled pork is typically made with fatty cuts of pork, but the moist heat of the slow cooker means you can successfully use leaner cuts, such as tenderloin, without sacrificing flavor. Here, I pair the pork with a sweet and tangy barbecue sauce made with fresh peaches. Serve this pulled pork as a sandwich topped with shredded cabbage, or ditch the bun and serve it stuffed inside Baked Potatoes (page 144).

2 peaches, peeled
  and diced
1 red onion, minced
1 cup sugar-free ketchup
½ cup apple cider vinegar
¼ cup pure maple syrup
2 teaspoons
  Dijon mustard
2 garlic cloves, minced
2 pounds pork tenderloin
2 cups coleslaw mix
¼ teaspoon kosher salt
6 whole-wheat
  hamburger rolls

1. In your slow cooker, stir together the peaches, red onion, ketchup, vinegar, maple syrup, Dijon, and garlic. Add the pork and turn to coat.

2. Cover the slow cooker and cook on Low heat for 8 hours.

3. Using a heavy spoon, stir the pork vigorously, coaxing it into shreds. Let the shredded pork sit in the sauce for at least 10 minutes.

4. In a medium bowl, stir together the coleslaw mix and salt.

5. Refrigerate individual portions of pork and individual portions of coleslaw mix in separate airtight containers (keeping the pork and slaw separate so the pork can be reheated easily) for up to 4 days, or freeze for up to 4 months. Serve the pork and slaw on the hamburger rolls.

⁜ **Prep Ahead:** In an airtight container, prepare the pork and sauce as instructed in step 1. This way, all you have to do in the morning is pour it into your slow cooker. Refrigerate for up to 5 days, or freeze for up to 6 months. If frozen, thaw the ingredients in the refrigerator overnight before adding to your slow cooker. Make the coleslaw, as in step 4, and serve as directed.

Per Serving: Calories: 395; Protein: 41g; Fat: 6g; Carbohydrates: 43g; Fiber: 6g; Sodium: 948mg

Beef and Broccoli

Serves 6 / Prep Time: 10 minutes / Cook Time: 8 hours (Low); 2 hours (High)

DAIRY-FREE FREEZER-FRIENDLY

This beef and broccoli recipe is so good that you might be tempted to delete your delivery apps. Cooking the steak all day in a rich sauce enhances its flavor and helps it tenderize. Oyster sauce gives beef and broccoli its classic flavor, but it can be loaded with corn syrup and artificial flavors. Look for an all-natural version, like KA-ME, and remember that a little goes a long way.

1 cup Beef Bone
 Broth (page 133), or
 low-sodium beef broth

2 tablespoons low-sodium
 soy sauce

2 tablespoons
 oyster sauce

4 garlic cloves, minced

1 tablespoon grated
 peeled fresh ginger

2 pounds sirloin steak,
 cut across the grain into
 ¼-inch-thick slices

½ cup water

¼ cup cornstarch

1 pound frozen broccoli
 florets, thawed

2 cups instant brown rice

1. In your slow cooker, whisk the beef bone broth, soy sauce, oyster sauce, garlic, and ginger to combine. Add the steak and mix to coat.

2. Cover the slow cooker and cook on Low heat for 8 hours, or High heat for 2 hours.

3. In a small dish, whisk the water and cornstarch until dissolved. Stir this slurry into the slow cooker to thicken the sauce.

4. Stir in the broccoli and brown rice.

5. Cover the slow cooker and cook on High heat for 10 minutes until the broccoli and rice are softened and warm.

6. Refrigerate individual portions in airtight containers for up to 4 days, or freeze for up to 4 months.

✳ **Prep Ahead:** In an airtight container, stir together the broth, soy sauce, oyster sauce, garlic, ginger, and steak. Refrigerate for up to 5 days, or freeze for up to 6 months. If frozen, thaw the ingredients in the refrigerator overnight before adding to your slow cooker. Add the slurry, broccoli, and rice as directed in steps 3 through 5.

✳ **Ingredient Tip:** Frozen broccoli is partially cooked, so it heats very quickly. If you use fresh broccoli, cook the recipe for 30 minutes more in step 5. You can also add fresh broccoli with the steak in step 1, but it will be very soft when cooked.

Per Serving: Calories: 340; Protein: 35g; Fat: 8g; Carbohydrates: 30g; Fiber: 2g; Sodium: 347mg

Korean-Inspired Beef Wraps

Serves 6 / Prep Time: 10 minutes / Cook Time: 8 hours (Low); 3 hours (High)

DAIRY-FREE FREEZER-FRIENDLY ONE-POT

Tender beef cooked in a spicy Korean-inspired marinade is one of my favorite dinners. I like to wrap the beef and rice inside a lettuce leaf or whole-wheat tortilla. Kimchi and sliced fresh cucumber add flavor and crunch. You could also skip the wrap and serve this meal in a bowl. Sesame seeds and fresh cilantro make great garnishes, whichever way you decide to eat it.

1½ cups kimchi, divided

4 garlic cloves, minced

1 tablespoon minced peeled fresh ginger

¼ cup sesame oil

2 tablespoons chili paste (optional)

1½ tablespoons low-sodium soy sauce

2 pounds sirloin steak

1 cup instant brown rice

6 romaine lettuce leaves or whole-wheat tortillas

1 cucumber, sliced

2 teaspoons sesame seeds (optional)

2 tablespoons chopped fresh cilantro (optional)

1. In your slow cooker, stir together ½ cup of kimchi, the garlic, ginger, oil, chili paste (if using), and soy sauce. Add the sirloin and turn to coat.

2. Cover the slow cooker and cook on Low heat for 8 hours, or High heat for 3 hours.

3. Using a heavy spoon, stir the beef, coaxing it into shreds.

4. Stir the brown rice into your slow cooker. Re-cover the slow cooker and cook on High heat for 10 minutes more, or until the rice is soft.

5. Refrigerate individual portions of the rice and beef, the remaining 1 cup of kimchi, the cucumber slices, sesame seeds (if using), and cilantro (if using), all in separate airtight containers for up to 4 days, or freeze for up to 4 months. Keep the lettuce or tortillas separate until ready to serve.

6. To serve, divide the rice and beef among the lettuce or tortillas and top with the remaining kimchi, cucumber slices, sesame seeds (if using), and cilantro (if using). Roll up the wrap like a burrito.

CONTINUED »

Korean-Inspired Beef Wraps *CONTINUED*

❋ **Prep Ahead:** Combine ½ cup of kimchi, the garlic, ginger, oil, chili paste (if using), soy sauce, and beef in an airtight container. Refrigerate for up to 5 days, or freeze for up to 6 months. If frozen, thaw the ingredients in the refrigerator overnight before adding to your slow cooker.

❋ **Ingredient Tip:** Kimchi is spicy fermented cabbage common in many traditional Korean recipes. Look for it in the produce section of most major grocery stores, usually near the tofu. It's typically sold in mild or hot versions, and you can use either for this recipe.

Per Serving (with 1 romaine leaf): Calories: 364; Protein: 38g; Fat: 17g; Carbohydrates: 17g; Fiber: 2g; Sodium: 438mg

---

Per Serving (with 1 tortilla): Calories: 503; Protein: 40g; Fat: 19g; Carbohydrates: 40g; Fiber: 6g; Sodium: 1,089mg

Thai-Inspired Barbecue Meatloaf

Serves 6 / Prep Time: 10 minutes / Cook Time: 8 hours (Low)

DAIRY-FREE FREEZER-FRIENDLY

When you think about it, a slow cooker is similar to a tiny oven—so why not make a meatloaf? This one is perfectly tender and juicy and is slathered with a spicy Thai-inspired barbecue sauce. Fingerling potatoes cooked right in the same pot make the perfect side dish. I like to serve this meatloaf with a side salad or with Ratatouille (page 136) for balance.

1½ pounds 93 percent lean ground beef

2 large eggs

½ cup bread crumbs

½ cup sugar-free ketchup

2 tablespoons low-sodium soy sauce

1 tablespoon sesame oil

1 teaspoon chili paste

1 chile pepper, thinly sliced (optional)

2 pounds fingerling potatoes

1. In a large bowl, mix the ground beef, eggs, and bread crumbs. Shape the mixture into a loaf and transfer it to your slow cooker.

2. In a small bowl, whisk the ketchup, soy sauce, oil, and chili paste until smooth. Pour the sauce over the meatloaf. Sprinkle with chile pepper slices (if using).

3. Arrange the potatoes around the meatloaf.

4. Cover the slow cooker and cook on Low heat for 8 hours.

5. Refrigerate individual portions in airtight containers for up to 4 days, or freeze for up to 4 months.

Prep Ahead: Prepare the meatloaf as instructed in step 1, transferring it to an airtight container instead. Complete step 2. Refrigerate for up to 2 days, or freeze for up to 4 months. If frozen, thaw the ingredients in the refrigerator overnight before adding to your slow cooker with the potatoes.

Ingredient Tip: Ground beef is simple, but if you're feeling adventurous, use meatloaf mix—a combination of beef, pork, and veal that's super flavorful.

Per Serving: Calories: 351; Protein: 30g; Fat: 11g; Carbohydrates: 31g; Fiber: 4g; Sodium: 632mg

Italian Meatballs with Zoodles

Serves 6 / Prep Time: 15 minutes / Cook Time: 8 hours (Low); 4 hours (High)

DAIRY-FREE   FREEZER-FRIENDLY

These hearty meatballs will make your house smell amazing. Use 93 percent lean beef because it strikes the right balance—it's not too dry and it won't make your sauce greasy. I like to serve these with zucchini noodles, but you can also turn them into meatball subs served on whole-wheat rolls.

2 tablespoons olive oil

1 onion, minced

8 garlic cloves, minced, divided

½ cup Italian-seasoned bread crumbs

2 large eggs, beaten

½ teaspoon kosher salt

2 pounds 93 percent lean ground beef

1 (28-ounce) can crushed tomatoes

1 (28-ounce) can diced tomatoes, drained

2 tablespoons tomato paste

2 tablespoons Italian seasoning

1 pound zucchini noodles

1. In a large skillet over medium heat, heat the oil. Add the onion and cook for 3 to 5 minutes until softened. Stir in half the garlic and cook for 1 minute. Transfer the cooked aromatics to a large bowl. Stir in the bread crumbs, eggs, and salt. Mix in the ground beef and form the mixture into 24 meatballs.

2. Return the skillet to the medium-high heat. Add the meatballs in a single layer. Cook for 3 to 4 minutes per side until browned.

3. In your slow cooker, stir together the crushed tomatoes, diced tomatoes, tomato paste, Italian seasoning, and remaining garlic. Add the meatballs.

4. Cover the slow cooker and cook on Low heat for 8 hours, or High heat for 4 hours.

5. Stir in the zucchini noodles. Let sit for 5 to 10 minutes, or until warm.

6. Refrigerate individual portions in airtight containers for up to 4 days, or freeze for up to 4 months.

Prep Ahead: Prepare the meatballs as instructed in steps 1 and 2. Transfer to an airtight container. Add the crushed and diced tomatoes, tomato paste, Italian seasoning, and remaining garlic. Refrigerate for up to 2 days, or freeze for up to 4 months. If frozen, thaw the ingredients in the refrigerator overnight before adding to your slow cooker. Add the zucchini noodles and finish the recipe as directed in steps 5 and 6.

Cooking Tip: Browning the meatballs before adding them to the slow cooker gives them more flavor, but you can skip this step if you're in a rush.

Per Serving: Calories: 387; Protein: 42g; Fat: 16g; Carbohydrates: 22g; Fiber: 5g; Sodium: 835mg

Salisbury Steaks

Serves 6 / Prep Time: 15 minutes / Cook Time: 8 hours (Low)

DAIRY-FREE FREEZER-FRIENDLY

The slow cooker works surprisingly well for this classic dinner of Salisbury steaks, potatoes, and peas. Dusting the beef patties in flour and browning them in a hot pan enhances their beefy flavor. Add the peas just before serving so that they don't overcook. I love serving this with lots of freshly ground black pepper.

½ onion, minced

2 large eggs

¼ cup seasoned
  bread crumbs

1½ pounds 93 percent
  lean ground beef

1 tablespoon
  all-purpose flour

1 tablespoon olive oil

1 pint cremini
  mushrooms, sliced

½ cup Beef Bone
  Broth (page 133), or
  low-sodium beef broth

1 tablespoon
  Worcestershire sauce

1 pound small white
  potatoes

2 cups peas

Freshly ground black
  pepper (optional)

1. In a large bowl, mix the onion, eggs, and bread crumbs to combine. Mix in the ground beef. Roll the meat mixture into 6 balls, then flatten each ball slightly to form a very thick beef patty. Lightly dust both sides with the flour.

2. In a large skillet over medium-high heat, heat the oil. Add the beef patties and cook for 5 minutes per side until deeply browned. Transfer the browned beef patties to your slow cooker.

3. Add the mushrooms, beef bone broth, Worcestershire sauce, and potatoes.

4. Cover and cook on Low heat for 8 hours.

5. Stir in the peas. Re-cover the cooker and cook on Low heat for 5 to 10 minutes until warm. Season with pepper, if desired.

6. Refrigerate individual portions in airtight containers for up to 4 days, or freeze for up to 4 months.

✳ **Prep Ahead:** Prepare the beef patties and brown as instructed in steps 1 and 2. Transfer to an airtight container. Combine the mushrooms, broth, Worcestershire sauce, and potatoes in a second container. Refrigerate for up to 2 days.

✳ **Cooking Tip:** If the gravy seems thin, leave the lid off the slow cooker after you add the peas; it will thicken slightly while the peas cook.

Per Serving: Calories: 321; Protein: 31g; Fat: 11g; Carbohydrates: 24g; Fiber: 5g; Sodium: 251mg

Barbacoa Tacos with Corn Salsa

Serves 8 / Prep Time: 10 minutes / Cook Time: 8 hours (Low)

DAIRY-FREE FREEZER-FRIENDLY GLUTEN-FREE

Barbacoa is a Mexican dish containing meat seasoned with chile peppers and spices that is cooked low and slow until succulent and falling apart. It's delicious as a filling for tacos or burritos, or on a plate served simply with rice and beans. Here, I use it in tacos topped with my favorite fresh corn salsa to balance the flavor and texture.

1 cup Beef Bone
   Broth (page 133), or
   low-sodium beef broth
5 garlic cloves, minced
1 red onion, diced, divided
Juice of 2 limes, divided
1 tablespoon
   ground cumin
1 tablespoon dried
   oregano
2 canned chipotle peppers
   in adobo sauce, minced
2 pounds beef chuck
   roast, trimmed and cut
   into 2-inch cubes
1 teaspoon kosher salt
1½ cups corn kernels
2 large tomatoes, diced
16 corn tortillas

1. In your slow cooker, stir together the beef bone broth, garlic, half the red onion, the juice of 1 lime, cumin, oregano, and chipotles. Add the beef and season with salt.

2. Cover the slow cooker and cook on Low heat for 8 hours. Shred the beef in the cooker and stir it into the sauce.

3. In a small bowl, stir together the remaining red onion, remaining juice of 1 lime, corn, and tomatoes.

4. Refrigerate individual portions of beef and salsa together in airtight containers for up to 4 days, or freeze for up to 4 months. Serve the beef and salsa with the corn tortillas.

✳ **Prep Ahead:** Combine the ingredients as instructed in step 1, placing them in an airtight container. In a second container, combine the remaining red onion, remaining lime juice, corn, and tomatoes. Refrigerate for up to 5 days, or freeze for up to 6 months. If frozen, thaw the ingredients in the refrigerator overnight before adding to your slow cooker. The tomatoes will break down and become saucier if frozen but will still taste great once thawed.

Per Serving: Calories: 329; Protein: 29g; Fat: 9g; Carbohydrates: 34g; Fiber: 5g; Sodium: 485mg

Ropa Vieja

Serves 8 / **Prep Time: 10 minutes** / **Cook Time: 8 hours (Low)**

DAIRY-FREE　FREEZER-FRIENDLY　ONE-POT

With the texture of pulled pork and the comforting flavor of pot roast, ropa vieja is a traditional Cuban dish featuring beef slowly stewed in a sauce of tomatoes, garlic, and bell peppers until it falls apart into shreds. It typically braises on the stove for several hours, making it the perfect candidate for the slow cooker. My favorite way to serve this rich dish is with a big portion of vinegary greens.

1 (28-ounce) can crushed
　tomatoes
1 green bell pepper,
　seeded and diced
1 onion, chopped
10 garlic cloves, minced
¼ cup fresh
　cilantro, chopped
2 tablespoons low-sodium
　soy sauce
1 teaspoon dried oregano
1½ pounds flank steak
¼ cup pitted green
　olives, chopped
Braised Collard Greens,
　for serving (page 137)

1. In your slow cooker, stir together the tomatoes, green bell pepper, onion, garlic, cilantro, soy sauce, and oregano. Add the flank steak and turn to coat.

2. Cover the slow cooker and cook on Low heat for 8 hours, or until the beef shreds easily. Using two forks, shred the beef in the cooker and stir in the olives. Let sit, uncovered, for 10 minutes to thicken slightly.

3. Refrigerate individual portions of beef and collard greens together in airtight containers for up to 4 days, or freeze for up to 4 months.

❋ **Prep Ahead:** In an airtight container, combine the ingredients as instructed in step 1. Refrigerate for up to 5 days, or freeze for up to 6 months. If frozen, thaw the ingredients in the refrigerator overnight before adding to your slow cooker, and add the olives as instructed.

Per Serving: Calories: 175; Protein: 22g; Fat: 7g; Carbohydrates: 8g; Fiber: 2g; Sodium: 480mg

Lamb Shawarma Sandwiches

Serves 6 / Prep Time: 5 minutes / Cook Time: 8 hours (Low)

FREEZER-FRIENDLY

If you've never had shawarma, you're in for a treat. This popular street food is typically roasted on a rotisserie, then shaved onto pita bread or a lavash wrap and topped with assorted condiments. Here, I've swapped the rotisserie with a slow cooker, resulting in super tender meat and a flavorful, highly seasoned sauce. Creamy yogurt-cucumber sauce balances the rich lamb and warm spices nicely—don't be tempted to skip it.

1½ pounds lamb
   stew meat
1 cup Beef Bone
   Broth (page 133), or
   low-sodium beef broth
1 tablespoon ras el hanout
1½ cups plain fat-free
   Greek yogurt
1 cucumber, shredded
2 garlic cloves, grated
¼ teaspoon kosher salt
6 whole-wheat pitas
Lettuce leaves, for serving
Sliced tomato, for serving

1. In your slow cooker, combine the lamb, beef bone broth, and ras el hanout.

2. Cover the slow cooker and cook on Low heat for 8 hours, or until the lamb is very tender. Using two forks, shred the lamb and let it sit in the sauce for 10 minutes to soak up the juices.

3. In a small bowl, whisk the yogurt, cucumber, and garlic to combine. Season with salt.

4. Refrigerate individual portions of the lamb and the yogurt sauce in separate airtight containers for up to 4 days. The lamb can also be frozen for up to 4 months. Serve the lamb in the pitas, topped with the lettuce, tomato, and yogurt sauce.

* **Prep Ahead:** Combine the lamb, broth, and ras el hanout in an airtight container. In a separate container, combine the yogurt, cucumber, and garlic; season with salt. Refrigerate for up to 4 days.

* **Substitution Tip:** For a gluten-free meal, serve the lamb and yogurt sauce over rice instead of in pitas.

Per Serving: Calories: 389; Protein: 33g; Fat: 11g; Carbohydrates: 41g; Fiber: 6g; Sodium: 625mg

Batch Cooking Staples

Chicken Stock

Serves 8 / Prep Time: 5 minutes / Cook Time: 8 to 10 hours (Low)

DAIRY-FREE FREEZER-FRIENDLY GLUTEN-FREE ONE-POT

I go through a ton of chicken stock, and making my own is more economical than constantly buying it at the store. You can use any type of bone-in chicken in this recipe. A combination of thighs and wings is my favorite, but I usually grab a family pack of whatever is on sale. Since this stock is unsalted, season any recipes in which you use it.

2½ pounds bone-in chicken pieces, skin removed

6 cups water

2 celery stalks, chopped

2 carrots, chopped

1 onion, quartered

4 garlic cloves, peeled

2 bay leaves

1 tablespoon fresh thyme leaves

1 teaspoon peppercorns

1. In your slow cooker, combine the chicken, water, celery, carrots, onion, garlic, bay leaves, thyme, and peppercorns.

2. Cover the slow cooker and cook on Low heat for 8 to 10 hours.

3. Strain and discard the solids, including the meat.

4. Refrigerate individual portions in airtight containers for up to 1 week, or freeze for up to 6 months.

Meal Prep Tip: This stock gets more flavorful the longer it cooks, so cook it all day—or cook it overnight while you sleep. This staple is used in Butternut Squash and Apple Bisque (page 44), Split Pea Soup (page 46), and West African–Inspired Peanut Butter Stew (page 51).

Per Serving: Calories: 55; Protein: 6g; Fat: 2g; Carbohydrates: 1g; Fiber: <1g; Sodium: 49mg

Beef Bone Broth

Serves 8 / Prep Time: 15 minutes / Cook Time: 8 to 10 hours (Low)

DAIRY-FREE   FREEZER-FRIENDLY   GLUTEN-FREE

Store-bought beef broth works well in a pinch, but it doesn't even come close to the rich flavor of homemade stock. This recipe has a big payoff for minimal effort. Broiling the beef bones intensifies their flavor and helps the broth achieve a rich brown color, but you can skip this step if you're in a rush. Skim off and discard any fat that rises to the top of the broth once it's been refrigerated.

4 pounds beef bones

1 tablespoon olive oil

2 carrots, cut into large pieces

1 celery stalk

½ onion, thickly sliced

4 garlic cloves, peeled

2 bay leaves

1 teaspoon peppercorns

2 tablespoons apple cider vinegar

8 cups water

1. Preheat the broiler.

2. Place the beef bones in a roasting pan and drizzle with oil. Broil for 5 minutes per side.

3. In your slow cooker, combine the carrots, celery, onion, garlic, bay leaves, peppercorns, vinegar, and water. Add the roasted beef bones.

4. Cover the slow cooker and cook on Low heat for 8 to 10 hours.

5. Remove and discard the bones and bay leaves. Strain the broth and discard any solids.

6. Refrigerate individual portions in airtight containers for up to 4 days, or freeze for up to 4 months.

⊹ **Meal Prep Tip:** As this broth is unsalted, season your recipes to taste when you use it. This staple is used in Beef and Broccoli (page 118), Turkey Swedish Meatballs (page 104), and any other recipe that calls for beef broth.

Per Serving: Calories: 45; Protein: 3g; Fat: 3g; Carbohydrates: 1g; Fiber: <1g; Sodium: 86mg

Vegetable Broth

Serves 8 / Prep Time: 10 minutes / Cook Time: 8 hours (Low)

FREEZER-FRIENDLY GLUTEN-FREE ONE-POT VEGAN

Store-bought vegetable broth can be somewhat of a gamble—some are super tomato-y and can make everything taste like minestrone. This garden vegetable broth gets its flavor from mushrooms and zucchini, so it has a more neutral flavor and a golden, chicken-like color that works in almost any recipe.

4 ounces white
  mushrooms, sliced
3 carrots, chopped
2 celery stalks, sliced
1 onion, chopped
1 zucchini, chopped
4 thyme sprigs
2 garlic cloves, smashed
2 bay leaves
6 cups water

1. In your slow cooker, combine the mushrooms, carrots, celery, onion, zucchini, thyme, garlic, bay leaves, and water.

2. Cover the slow cooker and cook on Low heat for 8 hours.

3. Strain the broth and discard any solids.

4. Refrigerate individual portions in airtight containers for up to 4 days, or freeze for up to 6 months.

✳ **Meal Prep Tip:** Use this in any recipe that requires broth. Or add cooked chicken, grains, or vegetables to transform it into a quick and easy soup. This staple is used in Savory Quinoa Breakfast Bowls (page 24), Mexican Street Corn Soup (page 43), Samosa Soup (page 45), Greek Stuffed Peppers (page 59), Tofu Fried Rice (page 60), Buffalo Chickpea Sloppy Joes (page 61), Sweet Potato Stew (page 65), Tex-Mex Quinoa (page 66), Root Vegetable Potpie (page 76), Pork Chops with Parsnips (page 110), Braised Collard Greens (page 137), and Mashed Potatoes (page 143).

Per Serving: Calories: 14; Protein: 1g; Fat: <1g; Carbohydrates: 3g; Fiber: 1g; Sodium: 14mg

Marinara Sauce

Serves 12 / Prep Time: 5 minutes / Cook Time: 6 hours (Low)

5-INGREDIENT FREEZER-FRIENDLY GLUTEN-FREE ONE-POT VEGAN

Marinara sauce is great for throwing together a quick pot of pasta or topping pizza or chicken Parmesan. I always have some in my refrigerator, and I keep a backup in the freezer. I try to avoid jarred pasta sauce from the grocery store because it can be full of hidden sugar and salt. This homemade marinara is simple, and you control what's in it. Plus, your kitchen will smell so good while it cooks.

2 (28-ounce) cans crushed tomatoes

2 (28-ounce) cans diced tomatoes, drained

¼ cup tomato paste

3 tablespoons Italian seasoning

1 teaspoon red pepper flakes (optional)

1. In your slow cooker, stir together the crushed tomatoes, diced tomatoes, tomato paste, Italian seasoning, and red pepper flakes (if using).

2. Cover the slow cooker and cook on Low heat for 6 hours.

3. Refrigerate individual portions in airtight containers for up to 4 days, or freeze for up to 6 months.

 ❋ **Meal Prep Tip:** Add Kalamata olives, capers, and red pepper flakes to turn this simple marinara into a zesty puttanesca sauce to serve over zucchini noodles. This staple is used in Italian Spaghetti Squash (page 62), Zucchini Lasagna (page 71), and Chicken Parmesan with Zucchini Noodles (page 89).

 ❋ **Ingredient Tip:** I love the texture that results from the combination of crushed and diced tomatoes. If you prefer a smoother sauce, use 4 (28-ounce) cans of crushed tomatoes and omit the diced tomatoes.

Per Serving: Calories: 60; Protein: 6g; Fat: <1g; Carbohydrates: 11g; Fiber: 3g; Sodium: 475mg

Ratatouille

Serves 8 / Prep Time: 10 minutes / Cook Time: 3 hours (Low)

FREEZER-FRIENDLY   GLUTEN-FREE   ONE-POT   VEGAN

Ratatouille is a delicious French vegetable stew made with eggplant, zucchini, fennel, and just enough tomato to make it a little saucy. It's also my go-to side dish—it seems to go with just about anything!

4 zucchini, diced

2 red or yellow bell peppers, seeded and diced

1 eggplant, chopped

1 small fennel bulb, thinly sliced

1 onion, chopped

1 pint grape tomatoes, halved

6 garlic cloves, peeled

1 teaspoon dried oregano

½ teaspoon dried thyme

¼ cup fresh basil leaves, chopped

1. In your slow cooker, combine the zucchini, red bell peppers, eggplant, fennel, onion, tomatoes, garlic, oregano, and thyme.

2. Cover the slow cooker and cook on Low heat for 3 hours.

3. Stir in the basil.

4. Refrigerate individual portions in airtight containers for up to 5 days, or freeze for up to 3 months.

* **Meal Prep Tip:** This ratatouille is a great way to add a serving of fresh vegetables to a heavier meal. Or toss some into rice, pasta, or an omelet, or serve it in a wrap with hummus. This staple makes a great side for Sweet Potato and Sausage Breakfast Hash (page 25), Pork with Pears (page 109), and Thai-Inspired Barbecue Meatloaf (page 123).

* **Ingredient Tip:** Red or yellow bell peppers are sweeter than green bell peppers and provide balance to this recipe. Plus, they look pretty.

Per Serving: Calories: 73; Protein: 3g; Fat: 1g; Carbohydrates: 16g; Fiber: 5g; Sodium: 29mg

Braised Collard Greens

Serves 8 / **Prep Time: 10 minutes** / **Cook Time: 8 hours (Low); 3 hours (High)**

5-INGREDIENT   FREEZER-FRIENDLY   GLUTEN-FREE   ONE-POT   VEGAN

Leafy greens usually don't hold up in the slow cooker, but collards are an exception—they're very tough when raw, so they're perfect for long, slow braises. This slow cooker recipe calls for a little more vinegar than most stovetop recipes because the liquid released by the greens dilutes its flavor. The greens can be bitter, so a dash of maple syrup brings balance back to the dish.

1 pound collard greens, tough stems removed, leaves roughly chopped

2 cups Vegetable Broth (page 134), or low-sodium vegetable broth

½ small onion, thinly sliced

2 tablespoons apple cider vinegar

2 teaspoons pure maple syrup

1. In your slow cooker, combine the greens, vegetable broth, onion, vinegar, and maple syrup.

2. Cover the slow cooker and cook on Low heat for 8 hours, or High heat for 3 hours until the greens are tender.

3. Refrigerate individual portions in airtight containers for up to 5 days, or freeze for up to 3 months.

❋ **Meal Prep Tip:** Try these greens on the side of Butternut Squash Macaroni and Cheese (page 75) or with Peach Barbecue Pulled Pork (page 117).

❋ **Substitution Tip:** Use kale or escarole instead of the collard greens.

Per Serving: Calories: 31; Protein: 1g; Fat: 2g; Carbohydrates: 4g; Fiber: 1g; Sodium: 177mg

Glazed Root Vegetables

Serves 6 / Prep Time: 5 minutes / Cook Time: 4 hours (High)

5-INGREDIENT DAIRY-FREE FREEZER-FRIENDLY GLUTEN-FREE ONE-POT VEGETARIAN

Have you ever craved roasted vegetables in the middle of summer when it's too hot to turn on the oven? Now you can make them in your slow cooker. No need to heat up your house or keep your eye on a hot stove. I love adding peppery parsnips and rutabaga to the mix to balance the sweetness of the carrots. Balsamic vinegar and honey make a delicious sweet and tangy glaze.

5 carrots, thickly sliced

3 parsnips, thickly sliced

1 rutabaga, diced

1 tablespoon
 balsamic vinegar

1 tablespoon olive oil

1 tablespoon honey

½ teaspoon kosher salt

½ teaspoon freshly
 ground black pepper

1. In your slow cooker, stir together the carrots, parsnips, rutabaga, vinegar, oil, honey, salt, and pepper.

2. Cover the slow cooker and cook on High heat for 4 hours, or until the vegetables are tender.

3. Refrigerate individual portions in airtight containers for up to 5 days, or freeze for up to 3 months.

   ❋ **Meal Prep Tip:** These vegetables go great with any meaty main dish—try them with Roast Beef (page 142) or Poached Salmon (page 141)—but I also like to pile them on top of a green salad.

   ❋ **Cooking Tip:** The vegetables will release some liquid as they cook; simply drain it off before packing them away.

Per Serving: Calories: 133; Protein: 2g; Fat: 3g; Carbohydrates: 27g; Fiber: 6g; Sodium: 251mg

Winter Squash

Serves 6 / Prep Time: 5 minutes / Cook Time: 6 to 7 hours (Low)

5-INGREDIENT FREEZER-FRIENDLY GLUTEN-FREE ONE-POT VEGAN

Winter squash is delicious, but it can be a pain to make. It's difficult to cut raw squash in half, and it needs to roast for a long time. Cooking it in the slow cooker solves both problems. You can cook it whole, then cut it open and remove the seeds once it's softened. Use your favorite hard-shelled squash for this recipe—I like butternut, acorn, and delicata.

3 winter squash

½ cup water

1. Add the squash and water to your slow cooker.

2. Cover the slow cooker and cook on Low heat for 6 to 7 hours, or until softened.

3. Carefully transfer the squash to a cutting board. Halve the squash and scoop out the seeds.

4. Refrigerate individual portions in airtight containers for up to 5 days, or freeze for up to 3 months.

✦ **Meal Prep Tip:** Serve squash with butter, cinnamon, and a drizzle of maple syrup, or cube it and puree it with broth to make a simple soup. You can also stuff the squash, as in Picadillo-Stuffed Acorn Squash (page 115).

Per Serving using 3 (2-pound) butternut squash:
Calories: 181; Protein: 4g; Fat: <1g; Carbohydrates: 48g; Fiber: 13g; Sodium: 20mg

Poached Chicken

Serves 6 / Prep Time: 5 minutes / Cook Time: 4 to 6 hours (Low); 2 to 3 hours (High)

5-INGREDIENT   DAIRY-FREE   FREEZER-FRIENDLY   GLUTEN-FREE   ONE-POT

Having cooked chicken in the refrigerator is so useful. You can throw it onto a salad, serve it in a sandwich or wrap, or even use it to make tacos or a quick stir-fry. I keep the seasoning in this recipe plain so that the chicken is highly adaptable, depending on what flavors you feel like having at the moment.

6 boneless, skinless chicken breasts

1 teaspoon kosher salt

1 teaspoon freshly ground black pepper

½ teaspoon garlic powder

3 cups Chicken Stock (page 132), or low-sodium chicken broth

1. Add the chicken to your slow cooker. Season with salt, pepper, and garlic powder. Pour the chicken stock over the chicken.

2. Cover the slow cooker and cook on Low heat for 4 to 6 hours, or High heat for 2 to 3 hours until the chicken reaches an internal temperature of 165°F.

3. Carefully remove the chicken from the pot and discard the cooking liquid.

4. Refrigerate individual portions in airtight containers for up to 4 days, or freeze for up to 3 months.

  ✳ **Meal Prep Tip:** Use this chicken for chicken salad, shred it and combine with your favorite barbecue sauce, or add it to soup.

Per Serving: Calories: 119; Protein: 24g; Fat: 3g; Carbohydrates: 1g; Fiber: <1g; Sodium: 603mg

Poached Salmon

Serves 6 / Prep Time: 5 minutes / Cook Time: 1 hour (High)

5-INGREDIENT   DAIRY-FREE   FREEZER-FRIENDLY   GLUTEN-FREE   ONE-POT

A lot of people I know are intimidated by cooking fish at home, but this salmon is nothing to be scared of. Cooking it gently in the slow cooker gives it a very soft, succulent texture that flakes into big, tender pieces. I prefer my salmon cooked medium, so I set my timer for 45 minutes; for more well-done fish, set it for 1 hour.

2 cups Vegetable Broth (page 134), Chicken Stock (page 132) or low-sodium chicken or vegetable broth
1 lemon, thinly sliced
2 shallots, thinly sliced
1 bay leaf
1 teaspoon peppercorns
½ teaspoon kosher salt
6 salmon fillets

1. In your slow cooker, stir together the vegetable broth, lemon, shallots, bay leaf, peppercorns, and salt.

2. Add the salmon fillets.

3. Cover the slow cooker and cook on High heat for 45 minutes to 1 hour until the fish flakes easily with a fork.

4. Remove the salmon from the poaching liquid.

5. Refrigerate individual portions in airtight containers for up to 4 days, or freeze for up to 3 months.

✦ **Meal Prep Tip:** Salmon is great reheated or served chilled. Use it to top a salad, combine it with Mashed Potatoes (page 143) to make salmon and potato cakes, or cook it ahead to make Pesto Salmon with Farro (page 85).

Per Serving: Calories: 153; Protein: 24g; Fat: 5g; Carbohydrates: 3g; Fiber: 1g; Sodium: 219mg

Roast Beef

Serves 8 / Prep Time: 15 minutes / Cook Time: 1½ to 2 hours (Low)

5-INGREDIENT   DAIRY-FREE   FREEZER-FRIENDLY   GLUTEN-FREE

Did you know you can use your slow cooker to make a roast? It's kind of amazing—and it's a great option when you don't want to heat up your house or when you have something else in the oven. It takes 90 minutes to heat the beef to an internal temperature of 130°F (medium-rare). If you prefer your beef cooked more, leave it in a little longer until it reaches a temperature of 140°F to 150°F. I don't recommend cooking it past medium-well because it can easily overcook when you reheat it.

1 (2-pound) top round
beef roast, trimmed
½ teaspoon kosher salt
½ teaspoon freshly
ground black pepper
1 tablespoon olive oil

1. Season the beef all over with salt and pepper.
2. In a large skillet over medium-high heat, heat the oil. Add the beef and cook for 3 to 4 minutes per side until deeply browned. Transfer the beef to your slow cooker.
3. Cover the slow cooker and cook on Low heat for Set 1½ to 2 hours, or until the beef is cooked as desired.
4. Remove the beef from the slow cooker and thinly slice it against the grain.
5. Refrigerate individual portions in airtight containers for up to 4 days, or freeze for up to 4 months.

❋ **Meal Prep Tip:** Roast beef is great served with a starch and a vegetable, or use it on top of a salad or in a sandwich.

Per Serving: Calories: 175; Protein: 26g; Fat: 7g; Carbohydrates: 0g; Fiber: 0g; Sodium: 705mg

Mashed Potatoes

Serves 8 / Prep Time: 10 minutes / Cook Time: 6 hours (Low); 4 hours (High)

5-INGREDIENT   FREEZER-FRIENDLY   GLUTEN-FREE   ONE-POT   VEGETARIAN

Nothing beats a side of creamy mashed potatoes. Russet potatoes tend to discolor when cooked this way, but gold or red potatoes stay a beautiful, creamy color. Their skins are thin, so there's no need to peel the potatoes. I like to cook the potatoes in broth and add a few whole garlic cloves for flavor.

2 pounds yellow potatoes, cubed

1 cup Vegetable Broth (page 134), or low-sodium vegetable broth

4 garlic cloves, peeled

1 cup plain fat-free Greek yogurt

¾ teaspoon kosher salt

½ teaspoon freshly ground black pepper

1. In your slow cooker, combine the potatoes, vegetable broth, and garlic.

2. Cover the slow cooker and cook on Low heat for 6 hours, or High heat for 4 hours, or until the potatoes are tender.

3. Using a potato masher or heavy wooden spoon, mash the potatoes in the cooker. Stir in the yogurt and season with salt and pepper.

4. Refrigerate individual portions in airtight containers for up to 4 days, or freeze for up to 3 months.

✳ **Meal Prep Tip:** Mashed potatoes can thicken when they cool. If you want, add a splash of milk or water when you reheat them to thin them.

✳ **Substitution Tip:** Use Chicken Stock (page 132) in place of the vegetable broth if having a vegetarian dish is not of concern.

Per Serving: Calories: 100; Protein: 6g; Fat: <1g; Carbohydrates: 23g; Fiber: 2g; Sodium: 238mg

Baked Potatoes

Serves 6 / **Prep Time: 10 minutes** / **Cook Time: 7 to 8 hours (Low); 3 to 4 hours (High)**

5-INGREDIENT   GLUTEN-FREE   ONE-POT   VEGAN

Potatoes come out of the slow cooker perfectly cooked, and baked potatoes are no exception. The insides get so soft and fluffy. You don't have to wrap the potatoes in foil, but I find it gives the skins a better texture and keeps them from getting soggy.

6 russet potatoes

1. Wrap each potato in aluminum foil and place in your slow cooker.

2. Cover the slow cooker and cook on Low heat for 7 to 8 hours, or High heat for 3 to 4 hours.

3. Let cool to the touch, then unwrap the potatoes.

4. Refrigerate individual portions in airtight containers for up to 4 days.

☀ **Meal Prep Tip:** Baked potatoes are great topped with chili or stew, such as Vegetarian 3-Bean Chili (page 48), Beef and Bean Chili (page 54), and Classic Beef Stew (page 55).

☀ **Substitution Tip:** This recipe works equally well with sweet potatoes.

Per Serving: Calories: 168; Protein: 5g; Fat: <1g; Carbohydrates: 39g; Fiber: 3g; Sodium: 11mg

Brown Rice

Serves 8 / Prep Time: 5 minutes / Cook Time: 3 hours (High)

5-INGREDIENT FREEZER-FRIENDLY GLUTEN-FREE ONE-POT VEGAN

I often use instant brown rice in my slow cooker recipes. You can add it right at the end, and it only takes a few minutes to steam. It can be expensive, though. If you prefer buying a big bag of long-grain rice, you can cook that in a slow cooker, too—it just takes longer. I've kept this recipe simple for maximum versatility, but you can replace the water with Chicken Stock (page 132), or stir in some fresh herbs for more flavor.

Nonstick cooking spray

2 cups long-grain brown rice

4 cups water

1 tablespoon olive oil

1. Coat your slow cooker with cooking spray. Add the brown rice, water, and oil. Stir well.

2. Cover the slow cooker and cook on High heat for 3 hours, stirring about halfway through, until the rice is soft.

3. Refrigerate individual portions in airtight containers for up to 5 days, or freeze for up to 6 months.

❋ **Meal Prep Tip:** Cooked rice freezes really well—I usually have a few small bags in my freezer. It's perfect for adding straight to soups. If you want to eat it as a side dish, add a few tablespoons of water when you reheat it to keep it from being too dry.

❋ **Ingredient Tip:** Adding a little bit of olive oil to the rice as it cooks helps prevent it from clumping together.

Per Serving: Calories: 185; Protein: 4g; Fat: 3g; Carbohydrates: 36g; Fiber: 2g; Sodium: 0mg

Beans

Serves 10 / Prep Time: 5 minutes / Cook Time: 6 to 8 hours (Low); 3 to 4 hours (High)

5-INGREDIENT   FREEZER-FRIENDLY   GLUTEN-FREE   ONE-POT   VEGAN

Beans are a staple in cuisines from all around the world, and they're so easy to make in a slow cooker. All you need to do is add dried beans and water, then cook until they're tender. You can add a bay leaf or other seasonings if you want, but don't add salt—it can toughen the outer shell of the beans and prevent them from softening.

1 pound dried beans
6 cups water

1. In your slow cooker, combine the beans and water.

2. Cover the slow cooker and cook on Low heat for 6 to 8 hours, or High heat for 3 to 4 hours.

3. Refrigerate individual portions in airtight containers for up to 4 days, or freeze for up to 6 months.

❋ **Meal Prep Tip:** As cooked, these beans are great to add to your favorite recipes. To enjoy them as a side dish, stir in a few tablespoons of your favorite salsa and a pinch of ground cumin.

Per Serving: Calories: 156; Protein: 9g; Fat: 3g; Carbohydrates: 29g; Fiber: 5g; Sodium: 13mg

Boiled Eggs

Serves 6 to 12 / **Prep Time: 5 minutes** / **Cook Time: 2 hours (High)**

5-INGREDIENT   DAIRY-FREE   GLUTEN-FREE   ONE-POT   VEGETARIAN

I'm terrible at making traditional boiled eggs—I either cook them too long or not long enough. As it turns out, slow cooker "boiled" eggs are nearly foolproof. This is one recipe that you want to keep an eye on, though—you'll want to immediately place the eggs in cold water after cooking to stop the cooking process. Letting the slow cooker switch to the "keep warm" setting so that you can deal with them later can result in overcooked eggs.

6 to 12 large eggs

1. Arrange the eggs in a single layer in your slow cooker. Add enough water to just cover the eggs.

2. Cover the slow cooker and cook on High heat for 2 hours.

3. Drain immediately and place the eggs in a large bowl of cold water to cool. Drain.

4. Refrigerate for up to 1 week.

❋ **Meal Prep Tip:** Boiled eggs are great as a grab-and-go breakfast, an easy snack, or a way to add protein to a vegetable-based meal.

Per Serving: Calories: 72; Protein: 6g; Fat: 5g; Carbohydrates: <1g; Fiber: 0g; Sodium: 71mg

Honey Corn Bread

Serves 8 / Prep Time: 10 minutes / Cook Time: 2 hours (High)

FREEZER-FRIENDLY VEGETARIAN

This corn bread has a higher ratio of cornmeal to flour than most recipes, giving it a nutty corn flavor and hearty texture. This bread is naturally sweetened by honey, which pairs beautifully with the corn flavor. I love mixing fresh corn kernels into the batter for even more flavor.

Nonstick cooking spray

1¼ cups cornmeal

¾ cup white
  whole-wheat flour

2 teaspoons
  baking powder

1 teaspoon kosher salt

¼ cup honey

¼ cup unsalted butter,
  melted and cooled

1 large egg

1 cup corn kernels
  (optional)

1. Coat a 6-inch cake pan that fits into your slow cooker with cooking spray.

2. In a large bowl, whisk the cornmeal, flour, baking powder, and salt to combine. Stir in the honey, melted butter, and egg to form a thick batter. Fold in the corn kernels (if using). Pour the batter into the prepared cake pan and place the pan in your slow cooker.

3. Wrap the slow cooker lid with a clean kitchen towel to trap condensation and cover the slow cooker with it. Cook on High heat for 2 hours, or until cooked through.

4. Refrigerate for up to 5 days, or freeze for up to 6 months wrapped in a double layer of plastic wrap and aluminum foil.

* **Meal Prep Tip:** This corn bread is great with soup or chili.

Per Serving: Calories: 199; Protein: 4g; Fat: 7g; Carbohydrates: 31g; Fiber: 3g; Sodium: 429mg

Whole-Wheat Dinner Rolls

Serves 12 / Prep Time: 15 minutes / Cook Time: 2 hours (High)

5-INGREDIENT DAIRY-FREE FREEZER-FRIENDLY VEGETARIAN

Dinner rolls might be one of the most surprising things to come out of my slow cooker when I was writing this book. I can't believe how well they turned out. The combination of white whole-wheat flour and honey gives them a sweet, nutty flavor; a little all-purpose flour keeps them light and chewy.

1 cup warm water

1 (.25-ounce) packet platinum yeast

3 tablespoons honey

1 large egg

3½ cups white whole-wheat flour, plus more as needed

1 cup all-purpose flour

1 teaspoon kosher salt

Nonstick cooking spray

1. In a glass measuring cup or small bowl, combine the warm water, yeast, and honey. Let sit for 5 minutes. Beat in the egg.

2. In a large bowl, combine the whole-wheat flour, all-purpose flour, and salt. Stir in the liquid ingredients. Using your hands, gently knead until a soft dough forms, adding additional whole-wheat flour if necessary. Roll the dough into 12 balls.

3. Coat your slow cooker with cooking spray. Add the rolls to the prepared cooker in a single layer.

4. Cover the slow cooker and cook on High heat for 2 hours, or until they reach an internal temperature of 200°F. Let cool.

5. Store in an airtight container at room temperature for up to 5 days, or freeze for up to 4 months, wrapped in a double layer of plastic wrap and aluminum foil.

Meal Prep Tip: Enjoy these rolls with your favorite soup, or use them to make a sandwich.

Per Serving: Calories: 172; Protein: 6g; Fat: 1g; Carbohydrates: 33g; Fiber: 4g; Sodium: 200mg

Measurement Conversions

VOLUME EQUIVALENTS (LIQUID)

US Standard	US Standard (ounces)	Metric (approximate)
2 tablespoons	1 fl. oz.	30 mL
¼ cup	2 fl. oz.	60 mL
½ cup	4 fl. oz.	120 mL
1 cup	8 fl. oz.	240 mL
1½ cups	12 fl. oz.	355 mL
2 cups or 1 pint	16 fl. oz.	475 mL
4 cups or 1 quart	32 fl. oz.	1 L
1 gallon	128 fl. oz.	4 L

OVEN TEMPERATURES

Fahrenheit (F)	Celsius (C) (approximate)
250°F	120°C
300°F	150°C
325°F	165°C
350°F	180°C
375°F	190°C
400°F	200°C
425°F	220°C
450°F	230°C

VOLUME EQUIVALENTS (DRY)

US Standard	Metric (approximate)
⅛ teaspoon	0.5 mL
¼ teaspoon	1 mL
½ teaspoon	2 mL
¾ teaspoon	4 mL
1 teaspoon	5 mL
1 tablespoon	15 mL
¼ cup	59 mL
⅓ cup	79 mL
½ cup	118 mL
⅔ cup	156 mL
¾ cup	177 mL
1 cup	235 mL
2 cups or 1 pint	475 mL
3 cups	700 mL
4 cups or 1 quart	1 L

WEIGHT EQUIVALENTS

US Standard	Metric (approximate)
½ ounce	15 g
1 ounce	30 g
2 ounces	60 g
4 ounces	115 g
8 ounces	225 g
12 ounces	340 g
16 ounces or 1 pound	455 g

Resources

DIETARY GUIDELINES FOR AMERICANS 2015–2020, 8TH ED.
A collaboration between the United States Departments of Agriculture (USDA) and Health and Human Services (HHS), this current body of nutrition, science, and advice on what to eat and drink helps promote health and reduce risk of disease. dietaryguidelines.gov/sites/default /files/2019-05/2015-2020_Dietary_Guidelines.pdf

FOODKEEPER APP
From the United States government, this is a resource that outlines food storage for maximum freshness and quality. foodsafety.gov/keep-food-safe /foodkeeper-app

HEALTHY DELICIOUS
Find more easy real food recipes on my blog! healthy-delicious.com

HEALTHY EATING ONE-POT COOKBOOK
101 Effortless Meals for Your Instant Pot, Sheet Pan, Skillet, and Dutch Oven. If you're looking for more one-pot, meal-prep-friendly meals, check out my first book.

SLOW COOKER OR PRESSURE COOKER
Kalyn Denny, a long-time food blogger, shares slow cooker recipes. slowcookerfromscratch.com

STILLTASTY
This is a guide on the shelf life of food. stilltasty.com

Index

Y

Z

W

About the Author

Lauren Keating is the author behind the blog *Healthy Delicious*, where she has been sharing easy weeknight recipes made with fresh, nutritious ingredients for over a decade.

Lauren studied plant-based professional cooking through Rouxbe cooking school and uses those skills to incorporate fruits, vegetables, and whole grains into her recipes in unique ways. She lives by the motto: If it isn't delicious, it isn't worth eating.

Lauren lives in Upstate New York with her husband, Shawn, and their two dogs. Get more recipes from Lauren in her first book, *Healthy Eating One-Pot Cookbook,* and at Healthy-Delicious.com. You can also find her on Instagram at @HealthyDelish.

CPSIA information can be obtained
at www.ICGtesting.com
Printed in the USA
JSHW040312210620
6287JS00001B/18

9 781646 118885